A YEAR WISER

365 DAYS OF INSPIRATION
TO CREATE A PHENOMENAL YEAR

Jill,

Happy Birthday, my friend.

Wishing you health, happiness,

CLIFTON ANDERSON

success and abundance!

Be Phenomenal,

Clifton

5/22/12

ANDERSON RESEARCH INTERNATIONAL

Los Angeles

A YEAR WISER

365 DAYS OF INSPIRATION
TO CREATE A PHENOMENAL YEAR

Copyright © 2010-2011 Clifton Anderson

Cover photograph taken by MacKenzie P Photography. Cover designed by Michael Durant of Imagine Depot.

ISBN: 978-0-61553-850-1

This book is dedicated to all those individuals
who endeavor to Live A Phenomenal Life.™

ACKNOWLEDGMENTS

I gratefully acknowledge and express deep appreciation to the amazing people who have made this book possible:

— To the many speakers, authors, leaders, actors, philosophers, sports figures, humanitarians, and others whose words have served as a continuous source of inspiration throughout my life.

— To my mentor and renowned motivational speaker, Les Brown, for urging me to pursue my purpose of inspiring the world through coaching, speaking, and writing. And thank you for suggesting that I change my voicemail greeting daily to learn new quotes. Who would have known that the discipline created in that daily activity would result in this book.

— To Maureen MacFarlane for editing this book. Your attention to detail never ceases to amaze me. Thank you for your diligence and your friendship.

— Most of all, to Mom, Dad, Chandra, Carlita, Phil, Phillip Michael, Cameron, Kennedi, Alana, my LP family, extended family, and friends for your support and encouragement. I cannot overemphasize the importance you play in my life.

FOREWORD

Get ready to take control of your life and live your best year ever! *A Year Wiser* provides 365 daily mind-expanding thoughts that will catapult you to your next level of achievement. This remarkable book is packed with breakthrough ideas that will inspire you to harness your personal power, achieve your goals, and manifest your greatness.

Clifton Anderson—highly sought-after results coach, author, and leadership strategist—challenges us to be conscious, deliberate, and disciplined as we go through each day directing our thoughts, sharpening our skills, and monitoring our actions in order to create the life we truly desire. Clifton is an extremely compelling and inspiring coach. He shares his extensive experience to teach people how to create the life of their dreams.

In his early development, Clifton showed innate signs of leadership skills and a sense of destiny that can perhaps account for his outstanding record of achievement. At the young age of 37 he became the Chief Financial Officer (CFO) of a billion-and-a-half dollar company. I say "young" because the average age of a CFO of a major company is 54.

In this, the first of many books to come, Clifton shares with us the thoughts, ideas, and life lessons that have influenced and inspired his highly accomplished life—a life that is still unfolding and soaring to even greater heights. Each page is written for you to take in, reflect on, and apply in various areas of your life.

Oliver Wendell Holmes said, "Man's mind, once stretched by a new idea, never regains its original dimensions." This book was written to release the power in you, improve your life, advance your career, and bring out the very best in you. That requires daily positive actions that become habits and evolve into rituals, which inevitably produce a year filled with personal growth and accomplishment. So center down and give yourself permission to go on this inward journey to your best year ever.

Les Brown

INTRODUCTION

In 2010, following the advice of my mentor, Les Brown, I began recording a new voicemail greeting each day. As an up-and-coming speaker, I agreed with him that this would be a great way for me to learn new quotes to include in future speeches. This story serves as a powerful example of how small steps can lead to a significant accomplishment.

The idea for this book came after I received countless voicemail messages from family, friends, clients, and strangers who heard my various voicemail greetings. The response was overwhelming:

- People told me that my "inspirational thought of the day" was exactly what they needed to hear.

- While I was out of town speaking at a conference, a telemarketer called to leave a message every day and called several times moments later without leaving a message. When she finally caught me at home, she explained that after hearing the thought for the day she had to call again so her co-workers could hear it.

- Then there is my Mom. At times when she called and I answered, she would say, "It's great to speak with you, but I was hoping to hear your inspirational message today." After talking for a while, I would have her call back and allow the call to drop into my voicemail, so she could hear that day's message.

Zig Ziglar once said, "People often say that motivation doesn't last. Well, neither does bathing—that's why we recommend it daily." All you have to do is read the newspaper or watch the news: we are constantly bombarded with negative events around the world. In your own life, you will experience upsets and setbacks. So it is critical to counter these events with uplifting messages and positive thoughts. That, in a nutshell, is the purpose of this book.

Years ago I decided to nourish my mind and spirit with inspiring books, tapes, CDs, and DVDs. The impact that this practice has had on my life is indescribable. I firmly believe that this has been a significant contributor to my success. Studies have shown that what you believe about yourself—your potential, capabilities, skills, and shortcomings—to a large extent will determine what you are able to accomplish.

Throughout the years, I have collected powerful and inspiring quotes. Even to this day, whenever I read a book and come across a great quote, I jot it down. When I am watching someone be interviewed and he or she says something that strikes a chord, I write it down. When I speak with relatives or friends and they say something profound, I capture the thought. In this volume, you will find the powerful words of philosophers, leaders, humanitarians, athletes, authors, and speakers, among others. For each quote, I share my interpretation of their words and explain how these expressions apply to everyday life. This book also contains original quotes, based on my own life experiences and many years of studying self development.

This book—with its 365 inspirational thoughts—was written in such a way that you can start reading it today; you do not have to wait until January 1 to begin. Over the next 12 months, I encourage you to read one inspirational thought each day. Take it to heart and reflect on it throughout the day. Then put it to practice. When you do this consistently, you can dramatically change your life for the better.

You have my very best wishes as you create your best year ever and Live A Phenomenal Life.™

1

Your potential is like the ocean. It is immense and extends beyond your ability to fully see it. It is wide and deep. It can be a powerful force. It has known parts and unexplored areas. Its surface is as far as most people will venture. By going deeper, you discover things that will amaze you. Explore the vast ocean of your potential!

2

Paul Martinelli said, "You are never too old to set another goal or dream a new dream." That is the right attitude. In 2007, at the young age of 95, Nola Ochs became the world's oldest college graduate. Never let your age deter you from getting what you want. Whenever you think it is too late for you to do something, remember Nola Ochs.

3

In the short run, it is easy to go with the flow, live in mediocrity, and do less than what you are capable of. But in the long run, life will prove more difficult. In the present it may seem hard to create a larger vision of your life, maintain a standard of excellence, stretch yourself, and strive toward big goals. In the future, your discipline will pay off. Do what is hard today...then reap the benefits.

4

Napoleon Hill wrote, "Cherish your visions and your dreams as they are the children of your soul—the blueprints of your ultimate achievements." What unrealized dreams are lying dormant within you? What goals have you yet to achieve? What potential plans await your time and attention? Breathe life into those dreams. Realize those goals. Execute those plans. And achieve amazing things.

5

Brian Tracy said, "You have within you right now, everything you need to deal with whatever the world can throw at you." It does not matter what happened to you in the past. It does not matter what obstacles you face today. All that matters is what you have inside. Within you there is possibility. Within you there is potential. Within you there is unimaginable power. All that matters is what is inside—so unleash it!

6

William Wrigley said, "If two partners in a business always agree, then one is unnecessary." This quote speaks to the value of getting different points of view. Surround yourself with people who share your objectives, but who think differently. When you are looking for a great idea it is much easier to find it when you tap the collective intelligence. Always encourage others to share divergent points of view.

7

Michael Jordan once said "Talent wins games. Teamwork wins championships." He was absolutely right. Though he is arguably the most talented person to play the game, the Chicago Bulls could not have won six NBA championships with Jordan alone. Your talent will get you only so far. If you want to accomplish truly great feats, assemble a strong team. Then just watch how much faster and further you will go!

8

Deep down within you there is a leader waiting patiently for the call to greatness. He is waiting by the phone for you to call. She is sitting by the door just waiting for you to knock. As Vince Lombardi said, "Leaders aren't born; they are made. And they are made just like anything else...through hard work." Awaken the leader in you!

9

The word vocation is derived from the Latin root, *vocationem,* meaning "a spiritual calling." Many centuries ago, a person's work was what he or she felt called to do. Imagine being so passionate about your work that you would be willing to do it for free. Today most people think of one's vocation merely as a way to pay the bills. Are you doing what you feel called to do or simply paying the bills?

10

Someone once said, "Adversity introduces a person to himself." When things are going well, it is easy to smile and maintain a positive outlook. But your true character surfaces when you are met with challenges and obstacles. It is during those adverse circumstances that people see what you are really made of. Who emerges when you go through difficult times?

11

Do not hoard your potential—it is meant to be explored. Do not shy away from your greatness—it is meant to be realized. Do not disregard your gifts and talents—they are meant to be shared. Do not deny your true self—it is meant to be expressed. Do not squander your opportunities—they are meant to be seized. Do not ignore your dreams—they are meant to be fulfilled!

12

Eleanor Roosevelt said, "Do one thing every day that scares you." You know that thing that you have been putting off. The mere thought of doing it gives you chills. It is when you stretch yourself that you truly develop. As you tackle the stuff that makes you uncomfortable, you grow bolder each day—ready to take on even bigger challenges. What scares you? Do it today!

13

Zig Ziglar once said, "Some people go around finding fault like there's a reward for it." There are people who only seem to notice the tiny speck on the new suit you bought; or complain about tomorrow's forecast instead of enjoying the beautiful weather today; or say how much they hate the "new car" smell. Surround yourself with positive, uplifting people.

14

What if a better way has been there all along? What if the optimal solution has been staring at you? When you are too focused on the *status quo* you can lose sight of possibilities. By limiting yourself to what is, you miss out on what could be. Be open to trying new things. Be open to considering outside perspectives. Be open to finding a better way. Be open.

15

Glade Byron Addams wrote, "Chase down your passion like it's the last bus of the night." When you are trying to catch a bus that is pulling away, you run, scream, and wave your arms. But when it is the very last bus, you go all out! You do not care what others think. Because you know your options are to catch the bus or take the long walk home. Are you passionate about what you do? If not, it can be a very long walk through life. Chase down your passion!

16

Some people are like a giraffe shopping for high heels. They were born with everything they need to be great. But because of something they read, something they saw, or something they heard, they think they need something more. Know this: You Are Enough! Everything you need already resides within you. So stand tall and be the magnificent person you were born to be!

17

Noelie Alito once said, "The shortest distance between two points is under construction." Sometimes when you are focused on quickly getting to your destination, you will encounter unexpected roadblocks and detours. Always remember that there is more than one path that will lead you to where you want to go. And who knows? You might just enjoy the new, more scenic route!

18

Dr. Martin Luther King, Jr. wrote, "Faith is taking the first step when you do not see the whole staircase." You may be tempted to wait until you have everything figured out before you venture out, but life never provides a clear and complete picture of the journey that awaits you. Have faith and take a step!

19

Words are simply words. Ideas are only ideas. Beliefs are just beliefs. Thoughts are nothing more than thoughts. What matters is what you *do*. Live by your words. Make your ideas a reality. Demonstrate your beliefs. Convert your thoughts into action. Don't just say, think, and feel. Do!

20

Og Mandino wrote, "I am here for a purpose and that purpose is to grow into a mountain, not to shrink to a grain of sand. Henceforth will I apply all my efforts to become the highest mountain of all, and I will strain my potential until it cries for mercy." You were born to be a mountain; not a hill, not a molehill, and certainly not a grain of sand. Make your potential cry for mercy!

21

Mark Twain wrote, "Let us endeavor so to live that when we come to die even the undertaker will be sorry." Imagine that—living in such a way that everyone wishes for you a long life, because you are giving, you are contributing, you are making this world a better place. Do not leave your legacy; *live* your legacy!

22

A word of encouragement. A warm smile. Doing the right thing. An all-weather friend. A peaceful night's sleep. Sunset on the beach. Fresh air. Uncontrollable laughter. Hope for a better tomorrow. In the words of Anthony D'Angelo, "The best things in life aren't things." Appreciate life's best things.

23

Les Brown said, "You can't see the picture when you're in the frame." Having the right perspective is tough when you are alone. Surround yourself with people who will help you see things you cannot readily see. They recognize your unique skills and abilities. They warn you about potential pitfalls ahead. Even someone who does not "like" you can be helpful in pointing out your blind spots. Do you get the picture?

24

Decisions. Decisions. Decisions. Life is full of decisions. Do not minimize the power you have to decide. There are countless alternatives in front of you. With each decision you make, you plant a seed that will reap some type of fruit immediately or at a point in the future. Decide with courage, wisdom, and integrity.

———◆———

25

Elsa Maxwell said, "Laugh at yourself first, before anyone else can." No one is perfect. Everyone makes mistakes. When you laugh at yourself, it helps in your healing. Studies have shown the health benefits of laughter. It also frees you, enabling you to move on. When you make a mistake, be the first in line to laugh. Trust me, others will follow…

———◆———

26

There was a story on the radio and the reporter mentioned that this smiling kid was eating a plain piece of white bread. The child's mother explained that they normally eat wheat bread. But because her son was especially well-behaved on that day, she decided to give him a treat. Imagine that—a slice of white bread as a treat! No jelly, just the bread. This story should remind you to count your blessings!

27

Regret is exhausting—it can lead to many sleepless nights. Regret hurts—it inflicts the pain over and over again. Regret is oppressive—it holds you down. Regret is heavy—it can seem as though you are carrying the weight of the entire world. When faced with regret: Accept responsibility, learn from the experience, move on, and commit yourself to living fully in each new moment. Live a life of no regrets!

28

We cannot change the past and we cannot predict the future. But we can control what we do today. Live life to the fullest today. Seize the day today. Make a difference today. Keep striving today. Live in the moment today. Dream big today. Believe you can today. Do it today! As Eleanor Roosevelt said, "Yesterday is history. Tomorrow is a mystery. Today is a gift. That's why we call it *the present*."

29

Oprah Winfrey said, "Life always whispers at first and if you ignore the whisper, life will eventually scream." Throughout life, there are seemingly insignificant events that serve as subtle messages. Perhaps it is people complimenting you on your gifts and talents or the constant reminder of your purpose. If you disregard the whisper, life eventually will grow impatient and yell at you to get your attention. What has life been trying to tell you?

30

Someone once asked the profound question, "Would you rather be right or happy?" In the answer you will find one of the keys to inner peace. Placing things in the right perspective helps you focus on what really matters. You do not waste time and energy on little, insignificant stuff. So the next time you are tempted to engage in an argument, ask yourself this question: *Would I rather be right or happy?* It works wonders!

31

There is a Chinese proverb which states, "Even the highest towers begin from the ground." Every great accomplishment starts with a first step. No matter how big your goals are…no matter how great your plans are…no matter how immense your dreams are. They all begin with a single step. Take that step today!

32

Everyone is destined for Greatness. But most people are not willing to pay the price it takes to get there. They stop well before reaching their destination. Some do not make it out of Smallburgh. Others settle in Justgettinbyville. Most just make it to Mediocrity. But you are different! You will endure the bumpy roads, traffic jams, and detours. Because you know that your destiny is worth making the trip!

33

James Conant wrote, "Behold the turtle. He makes progress only when he sticks his neck out." In order to get what you want out of life, you have to take risks. You must stretch outside of your comfort zone. Of course there are moments when that turtle pulls his head back into his shell…but he does not stay there forever. Stick your neck out and take some risks!

34

Whatever you call it… Let your hair down. Loosen your tie. Kick your shoes off. Live it up. Have the time of your life. Lose yourself. Stop and smell the roses. Take a break. Have recess. Do it just for the fun of it. All work and no play? No way! Enjoy your life!

35

Someone once wrote, "To the world you may be one person, but to one person you may be the world." Never underestimate what a profound impact you can have on others. There is someone who counts on you, perhaps more than you know. Through your words, attitude, and actions, you have the power to make a huge difference in that person's life. You mean the world to them!

36

When you free yourself from conventional thinking, something magical happens. Some of the greatest inventions were born out of creativity. From airplanes and automobiles to the Internet and smart phones. As George Prince said, "Another word for creativity is courage." Dare to be different. Be creative!

37

John Mason wrote, "You were born an original. Don't die a copy." There is no one on Earth quite like you. No one can compare to you. Three questions to ponder: Do you realize how special you are? Do you believe how special you are? Do you demonstrate to the world how special you are? Do not live your life trying to live someone else's life. Be you!

38

In a department store, I overheard a little girl say, "For every problem there's a solution" when she and her mother found an item that they had been searching for. Amazed, I asked her mother how old the girl was. She smiled and said, "Seven." Seven years old! Imagine the life she will lead with that perspective. Now imagine if you had that same attitude…

39

Elisabeth Kübler-Ross wrote, "People are like stained glass windows: They sparkle and shine when the sun's out, but when the darkness sets in, their true beauty is revealed only if there is light within." It is easy to smile and shine when things are going well. But the true test comes when difficulties arise—when you are faced with challenges and trials. Despite what you may be going through, make a conscious choice to shine your light anyway!

———◆———

40

Shhh… Can you hear that? There it is again! It is that still, quiet voice deep inside of you. It is whispering, but it speaks with such conviction. It knows your potential and has seen what you are capable of. It is telling you that there is more. It is yearning for you to step into your greatness. It is urging you to live the life of your dreams. Are you listening?

———◆———

41

Calvin Coolidge once said, "If you see ten troubles coming down the road, you can be sure that nine will run into the ditch before they reach you." How much time have you spent worrying about something that never happened? How many sleepless nights? When you worry, you waste precious time and energy and you rob yourself of fully living in the present. Simply acknowledge the risk, but refuse to become imprisoned by it.

42

Someone said, "Those who can't hear the music think the dancer quite mad." When you have a dream that others do not get, some will think you are nuts. But they do not see what you see. When you aim high, some may call you crazy. But they do not know what you know. When you commit to making a difference in the world, they might laugh. But they do not feel what you feel. Dance to your own music.

43

Life is not a popularity contest. There is no Olympic gold medal for a Most Liked competition. There is no Oscar award for Most Adored Actor in an Original Life. There are times to take a stand for what you believe in…even if it means sacrificing your popularity. Perhaps it is a cause that you are passionate about. Maybe it is holding someone you care about to a higher standard. Choose conviction over popularity!

44

Which team are you on? Those who settle for mediocrity or those who demand excellence? People who constantly complain or people who create the results they want? Those who stop at the first roadblock or those who always find an alternate path? The group that practices scarcity or the group that promotes abundance? Your team influences your dream. Choose wisely!

45

William Arthur Ward wrote, "Feeling gratitude and not expressing it is like wrapping a present and not giving it." One of the most fundamental human desires is to be valued and appreciated. Do not allow your appreciation of others to go unspoken. Give the gift of gratitude—today and every day.

46

Someone once said, "Experience is a hard teacher. She gives the test first, and the lesson afterwards." When life brings an opportunity or challenge your way, you must choose a response. But it could be days, weeks, or even years before you understand why it happened, extract the lesson, and finally "get it." Everything happens for a reason. Pay attention to life's cues and seek understanding.

47

Disappointment is a fact of life. It comes in many different forms. The key is how you respond. When things do not go as planned you must resist the urge to wallow in self-pity. A missed opportunity creates the space for an even better one. Curb your disappointment. Do not let your disappointment curb you.

48

Johann Wolfgang von Goethe wrote, "Look at a man the way that he is, and he only becomes worse. But look at him as if he were what he could be, and then he becomes what he should be." It is a blessing to have people in your life who encourage you. They see what is possible for you. They help you create a larger vision of what you could be. Always see people for what they could be. See people for their greatness within.

49

Ashleigh Brilliant said, "For some strange reason, no matter where I go, the place is always called *here*." That is funny, but also very profound. It is important to be present in the moment wherever you are. Perhaps this is why students are taught to say "present" or "here" when the teacher calls their name. You are always *here* so you might as well be present too.

50

Henry Wadsworth Longfellow wrote, "The best thing to do when it rains is to let it rain." There are some things you can control and others you simply cannot. Your ability to distinguish between them is critical for your happiness and wellbeing. Sometimes unexpected stuff will happen to you or around you. Your true power is always in your response. So let it rain!

51

John Maxwell wrote, "All leadership is influence." Leadership is not about you; it is about them. Leadership is about inspiring others. It is about transforming the world you live in. Leadership is about bringing out the very best in those around you. It is about having a vision that is larger than you. Leadership is about creating other leaders. It is about people marching toward a common objective. It is about serving others. Leadership...it starts with you, but it does not end with you.

52

In the book of your life, there is nothing you can do about what has happened. Those chapters have already been written and sent to the publisher for printing. But you can change the rest of the story. If you are not happy with where your life is heading, create a plot twist! Write with purpose, knowing that your story does not have to end the way it began.

53

Wayne Gretzky said, "You miss 100 percent of the shots you never take." No one can be guaranteed success without failures along the way. But one thing that guarantees failure is never taking action. Setbacks, mistakes, hiccups, and failures are all necessary ingredients for success. Take a shot! And if you miss, keep shooting!

54

Jose Ferrer said, "I am more important than my problems." That is the right perspective! No matter what challenges you face or situations you go through, always remember this: You are bigger, stronger, greater, more significant, more powerful, more resilient, and more important than any of your problems!

55

Attitude is everything. Your environment is a direct reflection of your attitude. An optimistic outlook enables you to see opportunities. A sense of perseverance allows you to become a victor over your circumstances instead of a victim of them. The type of people you attract into your life is based on your attitude. If you are ever dissatisfied with your situation, check your attitude.

56

Jacomo Casanova said, "Be the flame, not the moth." In life, lead by example. Do not be drawn to every shiny new thing that comes along. Be the type of person who attracts others to you and the worthy causes you support. Serve as a bright example who inspires others. Be the flame.

57

Someone once said, "Sometimes you win, sometimes you learn." You can learn invaluable lessons from a failed attempt. You learn about your character. You learn what commitment truly means. You learn how to keep going gracefully. You learn what does not work. You learn that failure is temporary. You learn that you are one step closer to success.

58

I saw a t-shirt that read, "My life is a circus without the tent." My first thought was that the back of the shirt should read, "...and I'm the ringleader." You have the power to create your environment—good or bad. You are the architect of your life. You can be the captain, the conductor, the CEO. Or, you can be the ringleader. It is your choice!

59

Po Bronson wrote, "There is nothing more genuine than breaking away from the chorus to learn the sound of your own voice." In so many cases people are encouraged to blend in instead of stand out. We are bombarded with ads, billboards, and magazines pushing the latest trends and fads. But there is nothing more liberating than being uniquely you. Find your voice!

60

Robert Jones Burdette once said, "Do not believe the world owes you a living; the world owes you nothing—it was here first." Feeling entitled to something without earning it is the easy way out. When you take full responsibility for your life you can exert greater control over what you get in life. The world owes you nothing, but you owe it to yourself!

61

Ivory Dorsey said, "The cat is already out of the bag. The toothpaste is out of the tube. And the egg shell is already broken. So you might as well make an omelet, brush your teeth and play with the cat." There are some things you cannot change. Focus on what you can change and make the very best of what you have.

62

Some believe that success breeds confidence. In other words the more successful you become, the more confident you grow. But actually the opposite is true—confidence is a necessary ingredient for sustained success. Confidence comes from within, not from external circumstances. With an unwavering belief in yourself, you attract talented people and ripe opportunities into your life. Be confident!

63

Norman Cousins once wrote, "Death is not the greatest loss in life. The greatest loss is what dies inside us while we live." It is believed that the average person uses no more than 10% of his or her potential. Ten percent! That does not even scratch the surface of your capabilities. You are blessed with a continent of unexplored gifts and talents. Use them, or lose them!

64

What is perfect? Perfect is the convenient excuse that keeps most people from doing what they know they should do. The perfect environment, the perfect circumstances, the perfect opportunity. These are all *perfect* illusions preventing people from living the life they are intended to live. Strive for excellence, not perfection!

65

Joe Girard once said, "The elevator to success is out of order. You'll have to use the stairs...one step at a time." He was absolutely right. Convenience and success have never occupied the same place at the same time. Success does not come at the push of a button. If you really want something, you have to work for it. You have to sweat for it. Make the climb!

66

Mark Twain wrote, "Twenty years from now you will be more disappointed by the things that you didn't do than by the ones you did do." *I wish I had...* is one of the saddest phrases ever spoken. Regret is a burden that is too heavy to carry throughout life. With each new day comes an opportunity to do what you have always wanted to do. No regrets!

67

What if it is true? What if your potential is far greater than you ever imagined? What if the stuff you have done so far is just the tip of the iceberg? What if your very best still lies within you? What if you have the ability to do some astonishing things? It *is* true. Now, what if you started believing that it is true?

68

Nelson Henderson once said, "The true meaning of life is to plant trees under whose shade you do not expect to sit." There is nothing like the feeling of doing something for others anonymously...a purely selfless act with no expectation of hearing "thank you"...with no desire for recognition. Commit a random act of generosity.

69

What extra baggage are you carrying around that you know in your heart you need to release? You should let go of those things that do not serve you. In order to receive the blessings intended for you, you have to make room for them. As Reverend Charles Mock said, "Many times, it's necessary to have a subtraction of a distraction in order to have a new addition." So what's distracting you?

70

Leo Buscaglia said, "Each of our acts makes a statement as to our purpose." Underlying everything you do and say is a specific purpose. Whether that purpose is spoken or unspoken...conscious or subconscious...meant to help or harm, every action you take supports it. Be deliberate about your purpose and ensure that your words and actions are aligned with it. What are your actions saying about your purpose?

71

Are you spending your time or investing it? When you spend, you do not expect anything back. But when you invest, you expect a return. Some people spend time doing mindless activities for countless hours every day. Others invest their time by growing and developing. Do not spend your time wisely—*invest* your time wisely!

72

Are you focusing on the finish line or the hurdles? There is something, deep inside, that propels you. There is something more important to you than anything else. No matter what challenges you face, it is worth overcoming them. When you focus on what truly matters, nothing else matters. Focus on finishing the race!

73

Viktor Frankl wrote, "Between stimulus and response there is a space. In that space is our power to choose our response. In our response lies our growth and our freedom." You cannot always control your circumstances, but you can always control your response. Use the space and choose your response!

74

Throughout history, mankind has explored foreign lands, the blue sky, the deep sea, and outer space. With each exploration, more questions are raised, knowledge is gained, and increased understanding is attained. But the greatest journey of all is inner space. Within you there is unimaginable potential, talents, and ideas. Explore your inner space!

75

How do you wear your success? Do you wear your success with excessive pride? Do you wear your success with a condescending look toward others? Do you wear it without acknowledging those who supported you along the way? Wear your success with humility, respect, and gratitude.

76

You have to admire the sheer determination of infants who cry when they are unhappy. Since they cannot speak yet, they use all the tools at their disposal to get what they want. Imagine the power you have as an adult to satisfy your needs, wants, and desires. Considering your access to vast resources—yelling and screaming not among them—anything is possible!

77

Sidney Poitier wrote, "I always had the ability to say no. That's how I called my own shots." Setting boundaries is key to living life on your terms. These boundaries should be based on the principles you believe in. When you are clear about what you want and what you stand for, saying no when necessary is easy.

78

Life is like a mosaic. There are smooth pieces and rough pieces…shiny pieces and dull pieces…delicately made pieces and others with ragged edges…colorful pieces and gray ones. Each piece serves a purpose and is connected to all the others. Up close, it is hard to appreciate their collective beauty. But when you step back, you can see the exquisite picture before you. Life is like a mosaic.

79

Bill Cosby said, "I don't know the key to success, but the key to failure is trying to please everyone." Let's face it, you cannot please everybody. Some people will not like you because of your smile, or your kindness, or your success, or your positive attitude. The fact is some people will not like you. When you accept this, it frees you and allows you to be true to yourself.

80

Meteorologists have the right perspective. They ground themselves in the current conditions: today's highs/lows. They briefly acknowledge significant events of the past: record temps. And they keep an eye on the future: five-day forecast. Honor your past accomplishments, live in the present moment, and look to the future!

81

Leonard Cohen wrote, "Ring the bells that still ring. Forget the perfect offering. Everything has a crack in it. That is how the light gets in." So many times people want to wait until they have it all together to do what they have always wanted to do...to do what they know they should do. Waiting until you are perfect means waiting forever—in vain. No one is perfect. Embrace your marvelous imperfections!

82

Sam Ewing once said, "Nothing is as frustrating as arguing with someone who knows what he's talking about." You have been there before...debating a topic with someone who clearly knows his stuff. What is it about human nature that makes people want to prove that they are right, sometimes at any cost? But wisdom is demonstrated when you listen openly, admit when you are wrong, and learn from the other person's knowledge.

83

Are you the cause or the effect? Are you the engine or the caboose? Are you making history or watching history be made? Are you the one everyone is talking about or one of those doing the talking? Are you the thermostat or the thermometer? Are you making things happen or waiting to see what happens? It is your life...play big!

84

Darren Jacklin wrote, "For every question you don't ask, the answer is no." So many times people do not get what they want in life simply because they do not ask. You will be amazed by how many things are negotiable. But unless you ask, you would never know. Ask the question…you might be surprised by the number of people who say, *Yes!*

85

Pssst! Hey you! Yes, you! There is a rumor floating around about you. I heard that you are amazing. I also heard that you are unique in every way. I heard that you have a vast ocean of unexplored talents. I heard that you were put here to leave the world in better shape than when you were born. So are all the things they are saying about you true? Ah ha! I knew it!

86

Jacob A. Riis wrote, "Look at a stonecutter hammering away at his rock, perhaps 100 times without as much as a crack showing in it. Yet at the 101st blow it will split in two, and I know it was not the last blow that did it, but all that had gone before." Success requires persistence, especially when progress is hard to see. Do not give up. Keep swinging! You never know when your break will come.

87

Think about all the artists and writers who died penniless, but whose works are now considered priceless masterpieces. Sometimes you can take for granted those who have had such a tremendous impact on your life. Whether family, friends, colleagues or acquaintances, why not show your appreciation while they are alive to receive it? Someone once instructed others to give her flowers while she is here to enjoy them and not to save them for the funeral!

88

Feedback is a gift. Sure, it feels nice when people compliment you. And you think, "Please, tell me more." But honest, constructive feedback is the most valuable gift you can receive. Who has been trying to tell you what you *need* to hear, instead of what you *want* to hear? Are you open to receiving the gift? Or does it just sit there unopened? And like any gift, the best response when receiving feedback is simply, "Thank you!"

89

Winston Churchill said, "We make a living by what we get. We make a life by what we give." There is nothing like the feeling you can get when you give to others. No strings, just giving. Imagine where this world would be if everyone were more committed to giving than getting. So are you making a living or making a life?

90

H.F. Ellis said, "An unwatched pot boils immediately." Have you ever noticed how quickly things seem to happen when you are focused on something else? Yes, I know you are amazing, but water will not boil any faster with you staring at it. Some things simply take their own time. Focus on those things you can control. For everything else, just let the water boil when it boils.

91

Laughter is power. When you laugh, you show that you are above your circumstances. When you laugh, you disarm tension and sneer at stress. When you laugh, you nourish your soul with natural medicine. When you laugh, you are choosing to be happy. When you laugh, you are saying that you know you will look back on this one day and laugh, so why wait?

92

Service is rendering habitual obedience to something or someone. Whether they admit it or not, everyone serves something. Even the most powerful people are serving something. It can be a belief, an ideal, a cause, one's family, one's country, or mankind in general. It takes priority over everything else. Serve something worthy of you and your service.

93

Howard Thurman wrote, "Don't ask yourself what the world needs. Ask yourself what makes you come alive, and then go and do that. Because what the world needs is people who have come alive." So many people sleepwalk through life. When you look into their eyes, you see that the thrill is gone. Life is short. Live it to the fullest. What makes you come alive?

94

Robert Frost wrote, "Two roads diverged in a wood, and I— I took the one less traveled by. And that has made all the difference." Heading along the path that most people take is a safe bet. But choosing your own route requires courage. Discovering your own way means making uncommon—and sometimes unpopular—choices. Charting your own course for your life is liberating. Be original. Pursue the path that is less traveled.

95

William Shedd said, "A ship in harbor is safe, but that is not what ships are built for." You were created to venture out into the world. You are meant to take some risks in life. You were born to live and learn. You can only discover new territories when you explore what is out there. Leave the harbor.

96

Mother Teresa once observed, "When I think I have a handle on life, the handle breaks." Life is unpredictable. Just when you think you have everything under control, life will shake things up. It will be something you did not see coming. While you cannot control many of life's circumstances, you can control your response. How you "handle" yourself when your "handle" breaks says a lot about who you are.

97

Step it up...you have been playing small too long. Climb higher...the view is amazing. Kick it up a notch...you know that you are capable of much more. Take a leap of faith...spread your wings and fly. Live fully...a cup is meant to be filled until it is full. Rise up...amazing things await you!

98

Steven Wright joked, "I bought some powdered water, but I didn't know what to add." That is funny, but it should remind you of people's tendency to overcomplicate things, causing them needless stress. There is power in simplicity. Many times the answer is staring at you, but you fool yourself into thinking that it cannot be that simple. But sometimes, it really is. Forget the recipe. Keep it simple.

99

Find your voice—you have years of experience and invaluable life lessons. Find your voice—your thoughts are only heard when they are spoken. Find your voice—when you are silent you rob the world of your insight. Find your voice—you have the ability to change people's lives with your words. Find your voice—you have a unique and powerful message to share. Use your voice!

100

Ralph Waldo Emerson once wrote, "In every work of genius we recognize our own rejected thoughts; they come back to us with a certain alienated majesty." How many times have you had a great idea, but dismissed it and failed to follow through? Then later you see that someone else made that idea a reality. Never sell yourself short. Your brilliant ideas come to you for a reason. Recognize your own genius.

101

This day is priceless. On this day, you can commit yourself to a life of excellence. On this day, you can choose a different course for your life. On this day, you can forgive a friend. On this day, you can stretch yourself. On this day, you can make a difference in someone's life. On this day, you can embrace your greatness. This day shall never come this way again. Handle this day with care.

102

There is an African proverb that says "If you have no enemy within, the enemy without can do you no harm." One of the biggest obstacles some people have to overcome is their lack of belief in themselves. With self-confidence, you neutralize the impact of personal attacks by others. Do not be your biggest enemy. Exude confidence in yourself!

103

Get over it...it has already gotten over you. Move on...the train has left the station. Let go...it has been holding you back. Turn the page...that chapter is done. Charge ahead...or get left behind. Drop it...and release the power it has over you. Stop looking in the rear-view mirror...you have vast possibilities on the open road ahead of you.

104

Someone once said, "A push will get a person almost anywhere—except through a door marked *Pull*." It is tempting to think you know exactly what someone else needs. Though well-intentioned, you can sometimes do more harm than good. Your actions could actually encourage the very behavior you hope to change. At times, the best thing to do is to let them pull the door open for themselves.

105

It is fascinating when kids reach the age when they ask *why*, followed by even more *whys*. But as people grow up, most feel the need to show others that they have all the answers. But answers are only gained when questions are asked. Curiosity and knowledge go hand-in-hand. Ask why. The answer might surprise you, change you, empower you, test you, awaken you, guide you, release you, propel you, or invigorate you.

106

Mahatma Gandhi once said, "The difference between what we do and what we are capable of doing would suffice to solve most of the world's problems." When you do not live up to your potential, you rob yourself and the world. You are endowed with a treasure of unexplored gifts and talents. They were meant to be used, developed and shared. Commit yourself to do no less than what you are capable of doing.

107

Which is bigger—your dreams or your reality? Do not try to shoehorn your dreams into your current reality. Do not allow your dreams to hide in the shadow of your situation. Do not let your dreams shrink and shrivel with each day that passes. Do not be held captive by your reality. Instead, be inspired by your dreams and make them a reality. Dream big!

108

Andre Gide wrote, "Man cannot discover new oceans unless he has the courage to lose sight of the shore." In order to achieve great things, you must be willing to take risks. You must be willing to step off of firm ground. You must be willing to leave that place where you find comfort. Without risk, there can be no reward. Lose sight of the shore!

109

Take a step. Step out of mediocrity and into excellence. Step out of scarcity and into abundance. Step out of complacency and into urgency. Step out of your past and into your future. Step out of playing small and into playing full out. Step out of comfort and into growth. Step out of distractions and into focus. Step out of revenge and into forgiveness. Step out of fear and into courage. Take a step!

110

Darren L. Washington, once said, "The sum of a man's life is the difference he's made in the lives of others." You do not even have to be good at math to understand that profound statement. This is what life is about. When you sum it all up, what difference are you making in other people's lives?

111

A visionary is defined as a person who is given to audacious or impractical ideas. Impractical ideas? The Founding Fathers of the United States were visionaries. Mother Teresa was a visionary. Thurgood Marshall was a visionary. Mary Kay Ash was a visionary. Henry Ford was a visionary. A true visionary makes the impractical possible. Be audacious and impractical!

112

Jim Rohn said, "Discipline is the bridge between goals and accomplishments." Absolutely nothing is accomplished without action. The number one reason that most New Year's resolutions are abandoned within a couple of weeks is lack of commitment. Without discipline, there is no real commitment. In order to achieve any objective, you must be disciplined and do the work. Build your bridge of discipline.

113

Dr. Seuss once wrote, "Be who you are and say what you feel, because those who mind don't matter and those who matter don't mind." How much time have you wasted trying to impress people who will never be impressed? It is extremely liberating to be real, authentic, and transparent without fear of judgment or rejection. The people who truly care about you will accept you for who you are. Just be you.

114

It seems some people have a Ph.D. in Problemology. Their sole focus is on the problem. They explore, examine, and explain it. They share all its merits. They discuss its sheer size. They bask in its glory. They know everything there is to know about the problem. And when you ask how they would solve the problem…silence. Imagine if all that energy were spent on finding solutions.

115

Someone once said, "Two wrongs don't make a right, but three lefts do." It is important to remember that there is more than one way to get to where you want to go. After you have chosen your destination and determined how to get there, you should be open to the fact that the journey might not go exactly as planned. There will be roadblocks and detours. The same is true in the journey we call life. When you cannot make a right turn, make three lefts instead.

116

Michael Jordan said, "I've missed more than 9,000 shots in my career. I've lost almost 300 games. I've been trusted to take the game-winning shot and missed 26 times. I've failed over and over and over again in my life. And that's why I succeed." When people think of Michael Jordan, they see the winner. They remember all the clutch shots. But behind every success is a series of failed attempts. Take a shot…and keep shooting!

117

Sure, you can be alone in the boat and row yourself across the lake. But you will move a lot faster with a group of people in the boat rowing in the same direction. You achieve so much more when you are supported by people working toward a common objective. That is when the multiplier effect kicks in. Who is in your boat?

118

There is a Jewish proverb that says, "What you don't see with your eyes, don't witness with your mouth." Can you imagine all the wasted time and energy that has gone into feeding the rumor mill? Whether it is true or not, it is much more productive to focus on your business, instead of someone else's.

119

How people respond when faced with adversity speaks volumes about them. Some people show up with an attitude...mad at the world. Others do not show up at all...hiding out and hoping that the problem will magically vanish. But some people show up with power and authority...realizing that they are bigger than their circumstances. When adversity knocks, how do you show up?

120

24 hours a day…everyone gets the same number. 24 hours a day…that is how many the world's greatest leaders, inventors, entrepreneurs, authors, and musicians were given. 24 hours a day…to be spent as you choose. 24 hours a day…to waste or invest. 24 hours a day…they expire at midnight. 24 hours a day…what could you possibly do with yours? 24 hours per day…what are you doing with yours?

121

Go on a living spree. While you are here, why not live it up? Make your list, then go be, do, and have everything you want. Live life to the fullest. Live a life of no regrets. Strive toward your potential. No restrictions apply. This offer is good for a limited time only. You do not want to miss this once-in-a-lifetime opportunity. Go on a living spree!

122

In music, there is something called a grace note. It is a little something extra…like the cherry on an ice cream sundae. In jazz, it is not a part of the original composition; it is just offered spontaneously by the musician. Imagine if everyone left a grace note. What if everyone did a little extra…just because. Imagine if everyone gave more than what was expected. Give a grace note!

123

Alex Haley wrote, "Find the good—and praise it." Giving sincere, positive feedback is one of the most generous gifts you can give another person. Deep down inside, everyone has a desire to feel valued and appreciated. Make a conscious decision to build people up instead of tearing them down. Praise the good in others.

124

Someone once wrote, "When you were born, happiness went around looking for you." You were born to be happy. Happiness is the most natural state of mankind. Unfortunately, most people tend to complicate things by making life more difficult than it has to be. Have you been hiding from happiness? It has been looking for you for far too long.

125

Ben Sweetland wrote, "Success is a journey, not a destination." Hills and valleys...curves and long, straight stretches...climbing uphill and coasting downhill...two-lane country roads and wide superhighways...traffic jams and lonely, quiet streets...potholes and freshly paved roads... scenic views and the concrete jungle. These are all part of the road of success. Enjoy your trip!

126

Your past can be a thief. It can rob you of experiencing joy in the present moment. Your past can be a liar. It will try to deceive you into believing that you can do no better than what you have already done. Your past can be selfish. It tries to hold on to you to keep you from uniting with your bright future. Put your past in its proper place...in the *past*. Live in the moment and create your future.

127

When an unforeseen crisis is added to your already busy life, it is tempting to feel overwhelmed. But no matter how big your challenge, remember that every great accomplishment began with a single action. In that first step is your power to direct your destiny. As Ralph Waldo Emerson wrote, "The creation of a thousand forests is in one acorn."

128

T.S. Eliot wrote, "You have to risk going too far to discover how far you can really go." When you take risks, you stretch yourself. You learn more about yourself when you take risks than when you stay in your comfort zone. When you risk, you may be surprised by how much you know, how talented you are, or how much you can do. So just how far can you go? Take a risk and see.

129

Others are living the life of their dreams. So why shouldn't you? They are creating the results they want. So why shouldn't you? They are living life on their terms. So why shouldn't you? They have nothing that you do not have within. So decide today to claim the life you deserve.

130

Mark Twain said, "Keep away from people who try to belittle your ambitions. Small people always try to do that, but the really great make you feel that you, too, can become great." If you think about your closest relationships, are you growing or shrinking as a result? Do they leave you feeling better or worse? In order to be great, surround yourself with great people.

131

Muhammad Ali said, "Impossible is just a big word thrown around by small minds who would rather accept the world they have been given than explore the power they have to change it." You have unimaginable power within you. So tell your seemingly impossible challenge to bring it on! Commit yourself today to creating the world you want. Use your power!

132

Ralph Waldo Emerson wrote, "The only way to have a friend is to be a friend." There is nothing like a friend who is with you through it all. This is what you look for in your friends, but it is also what you should be to them. In life's ups and downs, be the friend you would want to have. Be what the world needs...be a loyal friend.

133

Francois Gautier wrote, "Many live in the ivory tower called reality; they never venture on the open sea of thought." Your present reality is simply that...in the present. What the future holds is limited only by your imagination. Be open to possibilities. Be open to a new beginning. Be open to change. Be open to new horizons. Be open to different ideas. Be open.

134

Wil Rose said, "Success is not counted by how high you have climbed but by how many people you have brought with you." As you scale to the top, who gets to go with you? As you strive toward your potential, who is growing with you? As you transform the world, who is at your side? As you accomplish the unimaginable, who is with you? How many are climbing to the top with you?

135

If only… If only I had pursued my dreams… If only I had given my best… If only I had told them how much I care… If only I had taken a chance… If only I had followed my heart… If only I had made a difference in their lives… If only I had given more… If only I could have led a life with no regrets… Do not live a life of *if only's*.

136

A single smile changes things. A smile can alter the entire nature and tone of a situation. A smile could be just the ray of hope that someone needs when they have hit rock bottom. A smile melts the ice. A smile on the outside has the power to shift your mood on the inside. Keep smiling!

137

Ralph Charell wrote, "It is through cooperation, rather than conflict, that your greatest successes will be derived." You achieve so much more by working together toward a common objective. Extraordinary results are achieved. Synergies are created. Alliances are formed. Friendships are established. Conflict or cooperation…which are you creating?

138

Lisa Nichols said, "Your thoughts and your feelings create your life. It will always be that way. Guaranteed." Who do you think you are? Your thoughts become your reality. Whatever you think you are, you will do all within your power to prove yourself right. If you think you are a failure, you will sabotage your efforts. But if you think you are a winner, you will work to ensure your success. Think carefully!

139

Someone said, "If you think you are too small to be effective, you have never been in the dark with a mosquito." They do whatever it takes to survive. They can detect a target up to 18 feet away. They fly up to 150 miles in a lifetime—100 days. A single mosquito can have up to 3,000 offspring during its lifespan. If this small bug can do all that, how much more can you do not only to survive but to thrive?

140

The game is not over. It does not matter what the score is. It does not matter how tired you are. It does not matter what the commentators are saying about your chances. It does not matter that even your so-called fans are leaving early. It does not matter how hard it seems to go on. You have exactly what it takes to win this game. So keep fighting! Go all out! Play full out! Play all in! Play to win!

141

John Assaraf wrote, "The most wonderful gift one human being can give to another is, in some way, to make that person's life a little bit better to live." Making a difference in others' lives is not a chore. It is not a burden. It is not something you will regret doing. Each day, strive to make the world a better place and have a great time doing it.

142

William A. Ward said, "Adversity causes some people to break; others to break records." If you allow it, adversity can make you stronger. Adversity can stretch you. Adversity can test you. Adversity can bring out abilities you did not know you had. Adversity can propel you to accomplish amazing feats. So the next time adversity comes your way, do not let it break you. Instead, breakthrough whatever is in your way.

143

There is a Cherokee expression which says, "When you were born, you cried and the world rejoiced. Live your life so that when you die, the world cries and you rejoice." How will you look back on your life? How will others? Live a life by making a difference. Live a life with no regrets. Leave the world a better place than when you were born. Live a full life.

144

An old proverb states, "He who walks with the wise grows wise." The people with whom you choose to surround yourself speak volumes about you. They influence your beliefs, your habits, your priorities, your goals, your dreams, your perspective, your attitude, even your personality. So with whom are you walking?

145

Step it up. You were born to be great. Step it up. You are capable of much more. Step it up. There is more for you to do. Step it up. There is more for you to see. Step it up. There is more for you to be. Step it up. On top of the world the view is incredible. Step it up. Amazing things await you. Step it up!

146

Lisa Nicole Bell said, "Life is both too short and too long to do work you aren't totally passionate about." I heard someone suggest that the secret to happiness is to learn to enjoy whatever job you have. But I believe the true secret to happiness is finding what you absolutely enjoy doing and making a living doing that. It is your life, so demand more. Be unreasonable. Accept nothing less than that which makes your heart sing. Follow your passion!

147

People use surge protectors to safeguard electrical devices from spikes in voltage. Likewise, you need a surge protector for life—something that keeps stress from overwhelming you. It allows you to remain calm in spite of what you are going through. Do not blow a fuse; find your surge protector.

148

Lou Holtz said, "Don't tell your problems to people because 80% don't care, and the other 20% are glad you have them." Complaining only benefits you momentarily by allowing you to get things off your chest. But unless you are talking to someone who has the power to change the thing you are complaining about, it does not do any good. Change the stuff you can. For everything else, just let it go.

149

If they do not believe it, invite them to watch you achieve it. If they do not support you, make them wish they had. If they discourage you, find the inspiration within to keep going. Never allow others to define you, limit you, or deter you. They do not know your capabilities…but you do!

150

Potential is derived from the Latin term *potentia,* meaning power. So when people tell you that you have the potential to do or be something, they are saying you have the *power* to be or do that. This power can be exercised or not, but ultimately you decide. Exercise your power!

151

Dennis Miller joked, "I went to a bookstore and asked the saleswoman where the Self Help section was. She said if she told me it would defeat the purpose." While this is a bit extreme and funny, it makes an important point: some things you can only do yourself. No one else can do those things but you. You have capability beyond your imagination. Empower yourself. Believe in yourself. Be yourself. Help yourself.

152

Your past or your future…which do you choose? Would you rather dwell on irreversible yesterday or the possibilities of tomorrow? Would you rather focus on all the things you have done or all the things you could do? Would you rather be caught up in who you were or who you could become? Which do you choose…your past or your future?

153

Henry Ford once said, "Whether you think you can or think you cannot—you're right." You mindset is critical! Your belief plays a significant role in whether or not you achieve your goals. You can plant a seed of doubt or a seed of possibility. What ultimately breaks through the ground is determined by which seed you planted. So...do you think you can?

154

Exude naïve confidence. Laugh at the seemingly impossible. Have confidence in your ability to achieve whatever you set your mind to despite your current circumstances. Demonstrate an unshakable faith in yourself. Stare down all logic, the odds, conventional wisdom, and others' opinions. Be naïvely confident.

155

Confucius wrote, "Better a diamond with a flaw than a pebble without." When you wait for perfection, you needlessly delay the many contributions you can make today. You have more to offer the world as a flawed diamond than as a perfect pebble. Aim for excellence, not perfection.

156

Do not wait for permission to do what you know you should do. Have a burning desire to accomplish whatever you want. When you are passionate about your goals, you become unstoppable. When you have conviction and commitment, you can do anything. Take control of your destiny.

157

Do not give up...you never know how close you are to reaching that goal! Do not give in...you have worked long and hard to make your dream a reality! Do not throw in the towel...keep fighting for what you want! Do not punt...you are inches away from a first down! Do not wave the white flag...the battle is not over yet! Do not turn back...the view is worth the climb! Do not lose hope...keep the faith!

158

Life is a gift. How you live your life speaks to the value you place on this gift. Some people put their life on the shelf for future use. But life sits idly by. Others think "Well, it is the thought that counts." They minimize life's value, never fully appreciating its potential. But others accept this gift with care, realizing that it is the most valuable thing they will ever receive. What is the gift of life worth to you?

159

We are taught to believe that our friends will only say nice things to us. But a true friend takes a stand for you and holds you to a higher standard. Sometimes that means telling you what you *need* to hear. Like bitter medicine, their words can be tough to swallow, but you know that they are intended to make you better.

160

Press the reset button. When you work hard, it is important to relax periodically. Whatever you call it—recharge your batteries, take a breather, decompress, call time out, or regroup. However you do it—walk on the beach, read a book, go on vacation, get a massage, pray or meditate, or go hiking. So relax, then get back in the game with a renewed sense of energy and focus!

161

T. Harv Eker once said, "It's not enough to be in the right place at the right time. You have to be the right person in the right place at the right time." It is true that life sometimes offers second chances. But what if there is no next time? With every opportunity that presents itself, be prepared to make the most of it. Assume that the opportunity will never pass your way again. Pursue it with all your energy. Be ready…be the right person!

162

Samuel Grafton once wrote, "A penny will hide the biggest star in the universe if you hold it close enough to your eye." When you focus solely on small stuff, you lose sight of the big, important things. While details are critical, you should always keep the big picture in mind. The penny or the sun...where is your focus?

163

Dereke Bruce wrote, "In order to keep a true perspective of one's importance, everyone should have a dog that will worship him and a cat that will ignore him." There always will be people who simply adore you. In their eyes you can do no wrong. But there will be other people who could not care less about you. In their eyes you cannot do anything right. The key is not overreacting to either group.

164

Life rewards you only to the extent of your imagination. Set goals that scare you. When you dream small, you get small results. When you aim low, you shoot low. When you place limits on what you ask for, you guarantee a limited response. Be unreasonable. Dream big. Aim high. Ask without limits. Do not merely take it to another level. Take it to another dimension!

165

Ashleigh Brilliant wrote, "If you have something to say and say nothing, you are really telling a lie." So many people fail to speak up about the things they consider to be important. When you keep your thoughts to yourself, the world misses out on your ideas, your perspective, and your wisdom. Speak up!

166

Do not crawl to your goals. Do not stroll toward the life of your dreams. Do not saunter into your greatness. Do not meander toward happiness. Do not casually walk into creating your best life. Dash to your dreams. Sprint into fulfillment. Race toward your goals. Rush to your deepest desires. Dart toward excellence. Run to the life you deserve. Don't walk. Run!

167

They are two types of hound dogs: sight hounds and scent hounds. Sight hounds are taller and rely on their sight to hunt their prey. Scent hounds are short and close to the ground. They use their keen sense of smell to track their prey. These dogs use what they have to their advantage. If dogs have natural traits, imagine the far greater natural talents that we as humans have. Use your gifts!

168

Who are you when no one is looking? When others are around, it is tempting to play a role. The role of how you want to be perceived. The role of what others expect you to be. The role of fitting in with the crowd. But when there is no audience, the true you steps forth. Be uniquely you, no matter who is around.

169

Some people complain about being too old, while others believe that they are too young. Rarely do you hear someone say that they are the perfect age. The fact is, at this point in time, you are at the ideal age. Every day of your life has perfectly prepared you for the moment you are living right now.

170

William Ward wrote, "The pessimist complains about the wind; the optimist expects it to change; the realist adjusts the sails." There are many things in life we cannot control or influence. But some things we can control—our thoughts, behaviors, beliefs, and actions. If you are not satisfied with where you are, do not wait for the winds of change to blow. Instead, adjust your sails and change the course of your life!

171

Every journey begins with a single point. Perhaps you are at the point where you have had enough. Maybe you are at the point where you realize that there is so much more to life. You could be at the point of realizing that you have been playing too small. Or perhaps you are at a turning point and have a choice to make. Make the point and begin your new journey!

172

André Gide wrote, "Believe those who are seeking the truth. Doubt those who find it." There is always more to learn. Anyone who claims to know it all simply does not know how much he does not know. What a single person knows and understands is a mere drop in the ocean of knowledge, consciousness, and awareness. Be a perpetual student. Commit yourself to a life of learning. Keep seeking the truth.

173

Have you ever bought an electronic gadget that you used daily, only to discover weeks or months later that it had many more features that you never used? The same is true with *you*. You have limitless possibilities inside you. Realize your vast capability. Take a look within and discover how incredible you are.

174

Ben Franklin wrote, "If you want something done, ask a busy person." People who are typically idle can give you every reason imaginable explaining why they are not busy. But the people who can get stuff done are the ones who are already getting things done. In physics it is called momentum. Once you get going, it is easier to pick up more and more speed. Get busy!

———◆———

175

There is always more. When a marathon runner sees the finish line and knows it will be a photo finish, there is more he can give. When a singer has given her all, and her fans chant "Encore," there is more she can give. Just when you think you have done all you can, there is always more you can give. Call it excess capacity, reserve, headroom, or wiggle room. But there is always more. So give it.

———◆———

176

We can learn a lot from a car with a manual transmission. As you drive through life, you reach points where you have to shift gears. When your motor seems to be sputtering along, shift. Or when you feel the strain of your engine, shift. When life seems all uphill, shift. In order to go to a different level, you must shift! Shift your attitude…your perspective…your mood…your surroundings. Shift!

177

The thing that you push against can be the very thing that lifts you higher. Adversity makes you stronger. So when you are faced with challenges, stare into them. Know that—on the other side of them—you will be more resilient, more prepared, and more refined than before.

178

Long shot. Bottom seed. Fat chance. Underdog. Dark horse. Hundred-to-one shot. Tough putt. Ghost of a chance. Won't last through the first round. No matter what the odds. No matter what they are saying about your chances. Anything is possible when you first believe. Become the next Cinderella story.

179

How big is your Why? Your Why is the very reason for your existence. Your Why is the first thing you think about when you wake up and the last thing you think about when you fall asleep. Your Why should be big enough to cause you to run through a brick wall—simply because it is in your way. Grow your Why!

180

Ray Bradbury wrote, "Jump and grow your wings on the way down." Many times you learn what you are truly capable of when you are placed in situations that summon your inner strength. Taking a risk forces you to think creatively. It introduces you to skills you never knew you had. Take a leap and learn to fly!

181

What is holding you back? The world has been waiting for you. Waiting for you to be the magnificent person you were born to be. Waiting for you to realize your potential. Waiting for you to leave your mark. Waiting for you to live fully. Please do not keep us waiting any longer...

182

Did you check inside? Because everything you need you already have. Greatness is in you. Courage is in you. Joy is in you. Power beyond your imagination is in you. Peace is in you. Everything you need is within you...just waiting to be called forth. So when do your unlimited possibilities get to come out and play?

183

Lily Tomlin once joked, "I always wanted to be somebody, but now I realize I should have been more specific." There is something to be said about being clear about what you want. Your intention drives your outcome. Sure, the more general you are in stating your goals, the easier it is to meet them. But you are also much less likely to be satisfied. Be specific about what you want.

184

No matter what you are going through, keep your head up. When you are tempted to give in, keep your head up. When you are wondering what to do next, keep your head up. Keep your head up, because it will be easier to see your bright future when it comes over the horizon. Keep your head up!

185

Freedom to choose. Freedom to speak. Freedom to create. Freedom to reinvent. Freedom to live, love, and laugh. Freedom to excel. Freedom to be uniquely you. Freedom to relax. Freedom to learn. Freedom to pursue happiness. Freedom to prosper. Freedom to give. Are you fully exercising your freedom?

186

Who could have imagined it would be possible...to fly throughout the world...to fit thousands of songs in that little device...to have immediate access to a wealth of information over the Internet? All of these things are possible because someone first imagined them. Just imagine...

187

Marvin Phillips wrote, "The difference between try and triumph is just a little umph!" Sometimes the only thing that separates a successful accomplishment from a failed attempt is extra effort. So go back and tackle that problem again. Make another sales call. Pitch your presentation to another potential client. Share your book proposal with another publisher. Turn your try into triumph. Give an extra umph!

188

Grace Hansen said, "Don't be afraid your life will end; be afraid that it will never begin." There is nothing worse than a life full of regrets. One day... Someday... If only... I wish... I should have... I would have... I could have... Life is meant to be *lived*. Aim to be able to look back on your life and say to yourself, "Wow! What a life well-lived." Start living the life of your dreams now!

189

What good is a path that does not lead to your purpose? You are here for a specific reason. It is your responsibility to discover your purpose and to pursue it with urgency. No one else can do what you are here to do. As Howard Thurman once said, "The two most important days in your life are the day you were born and the day you realize *why* you were born."

190

Where did it go? That curiosity you had as a kid...where did it go? That insatiable desire to learn, do, and be more... where did it go? That unconquerable spirit...where did it go? It is still there. So awaken it. Embrace it. Demonstrate it!

191

John Galbraith wrote, "Faced with the choice between changing one's mind and proving that there is no need to do so, almost everyone gets busy on the proof." There is a fine line between conviction and stubbornness. When you are open-minded, you allow possibilities. You are able to explore options. You convey self-confidence by showing that you do not always have to be right. You enable your growth. You become wiser. Keep an open mind.

192

Charles Fletcher Lummis wrote, "I am bigger than anything that can happen to me. All these things—sorrow, misfortune, and suffering—are outside my door. I am in the house and I have the key." No matter what life brings to your doorstep, you have the power to invite it in for a brief visit, offer it a place to stay for a week or two, have it move in…or never let it in. It is ultimately your choice. You have the key!

193

Vince Toran said, "Intention drives attention." There is tremendous power in stating your intention. When you state your intention, you gain clarity about what is important to you. When you are clear on what you want, it enables you to focus. When you are focused, you empower yourself. When you are empowered you can do anything!

194

If you had the power today to define your legacy, what would it be? If you had the power to determine how you will be remembered, how would you be? If you had the power to change the world, what would you do? Well, you have that power and more. So how are you using your power?

195

Molly Ivins wrote, "The first rule of holes: when you're in one, stop digging." Yes, it is true…things really could be worse. Remember when you were faced with a problem that you attempted to "solve" only to find that you made matters worse. And the more you dug, the deeper the hole got. Sometimes the best thing to do is put down the shovel.

196

Ever wonder why cats have such quiet confidence? It is because they know what they are made of. They know that they are related to mighty lions, powerful tigers, and swift cheetahs. Inside of you, there is a lion roaring to be set free…there is a tiger ready to pounce on every obstacle that gets in your way…there is a cheetah ready to sprint toward the life of your dreams. Realize what is inside of you. Be a cool cat!

197

Henry David Thoreau wrote, "If one advances confidently in the direction of his dreams, and endeavors to live the life which he has imagined, he will meet with a success unexpected in the common hours." When you pursue your dreams with commitment and passion, amazing things will happen. Doors will open. Connections will be created. Opportunities will appear. Move confidently toward your dreams.

198

Ships, barges, canoes, rowboats, and motorboats all leave wakes behind them. You also leave a wake as you move through life. What type of wake are you leaving with the people in your life? A wake of negativity or optimism? Selfishness or generosity? Discouragement or support? Mediocrity or excellence?

199

Lewis Smedes wrote, "To forgive is to set a prisoner free. And one day you discover that the prisoner was you." Forgiving someone may seem hard. But living with resentment and anger is much more difficult. By not forgiving, *you* pay the most. You allow the pain to be inflicted over and over again. And you rob yourself of the joy you deserve. Forgive them…and free yourself.

200

Who are your background singers? With whom have you chosen to surround yourself? Together do you create a beautiful harmony or an awful discord? Is everyone singing from the same sheet of music? The people with whom you most closely associate have a profound impact on your outlook, your attitude, your self confidence, and your ability to make beautiful music with your life. Choose your background singers wisely!

201

Commitment is the capacity to keep charging forward in spite of the obstacles that get in your way. It is the burning desire to accomplish the goals you establish—no matter what. It is the ability to persevere regardless of what others think. So what are you committed to?

202

Michael Beckwith said, "You can begin to shape your own destiny by the attitude that you keep." You have more control over your circumstances than perhaps you realize. You have remarkable power to change your situation. Your destiny begins with your attitude and with each choice you make. Shape your destiny with intention.

203

What are you waiting for? The can opener was invented roughly 50 years after the metal can. What problem is waiting for your solution? What brilliant idea do you need to make a reality? What inventions are you holding on to? What books have you yet to write? What masterpieces are yearning for you to pick up the paintbrush? What songs await your voice? What are you waiting for?

204

Your story is an original. Share it. You have gained invaluable lessons. Teach them. You made some mistakes along the way. Move past them. You have accomplished some great things. Outdo them. Your life can be spectacular. Live it!

205

Andre Guess wrote, "Give a man what he wants but not what he needs and he will go away happy. But he might return and blame you that he doesn't have what he needs. Give a man what he needs but doesn't want and he may go away dissatisfied. But he will soon return with thanksgiving." Many people prioritize their wants over their needs, but the pleasure is always short-lived. It takes courage to give people what they need instead of what they want.

206

There is something to be said for a completed project: all of the tasks checked off...all of the activities completed...all of the obstacles overcome...all of the open items closed. How many unfinished projects do you have waiting for your attention? So what is stopping you? *You!* Experience the satisfying feeling of a job well done. Finish the job.

207

If you only knew… If you only knew the full extent of your potential. If you only knew what an incredible person you are. If you only knew the greatness that resides within you. If you only knew the abundance of gifts and talents you possess. If you only knew the vast power that you hold inside. If you only knew how you could transform the world. If you only knew…

208

Many do just enough to get by—few demand the most out of life. Many accept their circumstances as a given—few create the environment they desire. Many blame others for their problems—few take responsibility for their lives. Many believe success happens to the lucky—few know success is created through hard work. Many see obstacles—few see opportunities. Many or few…which are you?

209

Ambrose Redmoon wrote, "Courage is not the absence of fear, but rather the judgment that something else is more important than fear." People have overcome all types of fear. In each case there is something on the other side of the fear that overshadows that fear. Something is worth breaking through the fear you experience. Decide what is more important.

210

A true leader understands that he serves the people who are a part of his organization or family. A true leader creates an environment in which her team can excel and she expects them to do so. A true leader eliminates the barriers that his team faces. Be a true leader!

211

Voltaire wrote, "Every man is guilty of all the good he didn't do." Everyone has something to offer. By failing to do what you are capable of, you rob everyone. Imagine if each person had a burning desire to leave the world in better shape than they found it. What good are you doing?

212

You are ready. You are ready to take on the world. You are ready to accomplish extraordinary things. You are ready to live your greatest life. You are ready to create your destiny. You are ready to break down any barrier that gets in your way. You are ready to be the magnificent person you were designed to be. You were born ready!

213

Are you willing to do whatever it takes to reach your goals? Are you willing to tune out the naysayers? Are you willing to withstand the funny looks? Are you willing to work diligently to enjoy the life you deserve? Be willing to do whatever it takes. Your destination is worth that journey.

214

Stopped at a traffic light, there was an SUV with the words "Hi Mommy!" handwritten on the dirty back window. The words were written backward, so each time the driver looked in her rear-view mirror, she saw this special message from her child. How refreshing to see this instead of the predictable "Wash me!" That little kid chose to send a different message. What message are you sending?

215

Winston Churchill said, "When you're going through hell, keep going!" The worst time to stop is when things are at their worst. So keep going! It is when life is most difficult that you must refuse to give up. So keep going! When you are tempted to give in, give it all you have. No matter what you are going through, keep going!

216

Greg S. Reid wrote, "In the end, the extent of our own success will be measured by the accomplishments we have helped create in others." There are few feelings more gratifying than helping someone achieve their goals. Mentor someone. Empower someone. Guide someone. Support someone. Challenge someone into their greatness. It is true that the more you give, the more you get.

217

Bishop Charles E. Blake said, "Inactivity is the junkyard of dreams." It is critical to know what you want and where you are going. But unless your dreams and plans are followed by action, they do not amount to much. If you fail to act, you ensure that you will never reach your desired destination. Don't just sit there!

218

Create an anti-dumping zone. Do not allow chronically negative people to dump their thoughts into your mind. Do not let others smother your dreams with their wet blanket. Do not allow those around you to infect you with their mad-at-the-world attitude. Never let their *you can't* overpower your *I can.*

219

Edmund Hillary wrote, "It is not the mountain we conquer but ourselves." Your biggest barrier to success can sometimes be you, yourself. Within you is the power to overcome every obstacle—inside and out. Conquer your fears. Conquer your past. Conquer your doubts. Conquer negativity. Conquer self-imposed limitations. Conquer yourself…then conquer your mountain!

220

Years from now, do not ask the question: What could I have been? Instead ask yourself today, What might I become? It is not too late to change the course of your life. You have the power to create your destiny. The extent of your potential is unimaginable. Explore it, develop it, and become it!

221

Richard Bach wrote, "Here is a test to find whether your mission on earth is finished: If you're alive it isn't." You came here for a reason. You arrived with a specific assignment. You are here to pursue your purpose. Pursue your purpose with intention. Pursue your purpose with passion. Pursue your purpose with intensity. Are you still here? Then you still have work to do.

222

My friend, Pauline Victoria Aughe, inspires and amazes me. Pauline was born without arms or legs. We met at a seminar and sat next to each other. Like most participants Pauline was taking notes. But she uses her mouth to secure her pen and write. At one point, I glanced down and noticed that her writing was neater than mine! Absolutely perfect penmanship. She swims, drives, and gave birth to a wonderful son. Pauline accepts nothing but her best. What's your excuse?

223

Colin Powell once said, "Don't take counsel from your fears." Fear will advise you to stay in your comfort zone. Fear will caution you not to take any risks. Fear will lure you into complacency. Fear will try to convince you to play small. While everyone experiences some level of fear, it is critical to put your fear in its proper place. Do not listen to your fears.

224

Albert Camus wrote, "In the depth of winter, I finally learned that within me lay an invincible summer." Just as sure as the seasons change, know that you have exactly what you need to overcome any challenge that comes your way. Sometimes you have to go through adversity to realize the vast power that you have within. Within you is an invincible summer!

225

Anger does not deserve you. Mediocrity does not deserve you. Sadness does not deserve you. Fear does not deserve you. Negativism does not deserve you. They have not earned the right to claim you. Rather, you deserve happiness. You deserve excellence. You deserve a fulfilled life. You deserve peace. You deserve success...however you define it. You deserve greatness. You deserve it all. Go get it!

226

Magic Johnson said, "All kids need a little help, a little hope, and someone who believes in them." Do not underestimate the impact you can have on a child. Every word—good or bad—spoken to a child is amplified and stays with them for years. The potential that each kid possesses is immense. With the right environment, he or she can be and do anything. Encourage every child you meet.

227

Life is made up of each moment you live; each minute, each hour, each day, each week, each year. In wasting time you waste your very life. Be clear about what you are trading your life for. Every second counts. Live intentionally. Live with zest. Live full out. Live like you mean it. *Carpe diem!* Seize the day!

228

There is an Italian expression which says, "Once the game is over, the king and the pawn go back into the same box." This is as true in the game of chess as it is in life. Everyone is human, no matter where they find themselves in life. Everyone deserves to be treated with dignity and respect.

229

What is more important? If you are not living or creating the life of your dreams, then something else must be more important. So what is it... Comfort? Convenience? Living in the past? Fear? Desire to fit in? Daily tasks? Settling for less? Nothing should be more important than making your dreams a reality.

230

David Allen said, "You can do anything, but not everything." We have the ability to do anything we set our minds to doing—big and small things. This requires a clear intention, commitment, dedication, and perseverance. But there is tremendous power in focusing our efforts on the stuff that really matters—on the critical few instead of the trivial many, according to Pareto's Law.

231

Jack Canfield wrote, "Most everything that you want is just outside your comfort zone." It is one of life's biggest tragedies—people settling for less than what they are capable of. You deserve to live the life of your dreams. Stretch yourself. Demand more out of life. Aim high. Step beyond your comfort zone.

232

Years ago, I heard a phrase that has had a profound impact on my life: Change before you have to. When you anticipate what is coming over the horizon, make the necessary changes early. Be a victor over changing circumstances instead of a victim. Do not play catch up…be the one others are trying to catch up with.

233

Publilius Syrus said, "No pleasure lasts if it is unseasoned by variety." There really is too much of a good thing. Shake things up. Ask what if... Take the scenic route to work. Order dessert first. Learn a new skill. Meet some new friends. Learn a different language. Read a book that you would *never* read. Add variety to your life!

234

Do not just sit back and settle for mediocrity. Lean forward and commit to excellence. Lean forward and demand more out of life. Lean forward and pursue your greatness. Lean forward and discover your true purpose. Lean forward and accept nothing less than your absolute best. Do not sit back. Lean forward!

235

Michael Strasner said, "If the sky is the limit, how high is your sky?" Many of the barriers people face, they have created themselves. Most of the limits you bump up against are self-imposed. You are constrained only by your imagination. Be outrageous. Think big. Raise the roof on your sky.

236

Winston Churchill once said, "Never, never, never, never give up!" Giving up is alluring. Admitting defeat is easy. Calling it quits is simple. Waving the white flag can be appealing. But few characteristics are as noble as persistence. Have the tenacity to keep going until you are finished. Be stubbornly committed to your goals. Never give up!

237

Never mistake knowledge for wisdom. Knowledge can be measured on an exam. Wisdom only can be measured in real life. Knowledge is academic. Wisdom is practical. Knowledge determines how you think. Wisdom determines how you act. Knowledge will only take you so far in life. With wisdom, the possibilities are limitless. Do not settle for knowledge. Seek wisdom.

238

Alexander Graham Bell said, "When one door closes, another one opens. But we often look so long and so regretfully upon the closed door that we do not see the one which has opened for us." By dwelling on yesterday's failures we miss tomorrow's blessings. Stop looking at that old door and shift your attention to the new one opening before you.

239

There is incremental change; then there is transformation. Both result in change. However, incremental change is evolutionary; transformation is a revolutionary change. Incremental change is marginal; transformation is dramatic. If you really want it, be bold and unreasonable. Transform yourself, your life, and your world!

240

Someone once said, "Every survival kit should include a sense of humor." Imagine a life without laughter. When you take yourself too seriously you rob yourself of many of life's joyous moments. Add a dose of humor to your survival kit.

241

Someone once said, "Peace. It does not mean to be in a place where there is no noise, trouble or hard work. It means to be in the midst of those things and still be calm in your heart." In the middle of the chaos, find your peace. When you lose something important to you, find your peace. When life throws you a curve ball, find your peace. No matter what is going on around you, find your peace.

242

"It takes courage to grow up and become who you really are." Those are the words of e.e. cummings. What if the person you were born to be still lies within you waiting to be awakened? What if you have been playing a role? What if your most magnificent self is being held hostage? Remember the person you always wanted to be. Become who you really are.

243

Someone once said, "Just when the caterpillar thought the world was over, it became a butterfly." Sometimes the unimaginable happens to you. But no matter what challenges you face, keep going. You are resilient. You are unstoppable. You have an unconquerable spirit. You are a force to be reckoned with. You were born to shine. So keep going, because your destiny awaits…

244

How do you plead? Are you guilty of playing at a level that is well below your capability? Are you guilty of shying away from your potential? Are you guilty of stopping just short of realizing your greatness? Are you guilty of settling for less than you deserve? Are you guilty of trying to put off your future? Do not be guilty!

245

Ruth E. Renkel once said, "Never fear shadows. They simply mean there's a light shining somewhere nearby." No matter how bad it gets, always remember that things will get better. No matter how much you want to throw up your hands in defeat, never give up. No matter how dark it might appear, know that at the end of every dark period there is light.

246

W.M. Lewis said, "The tragedy of life is not that it ends so soon, but that we wait so long to begin it." What are you waiting for? Commit yourself to living your best life *here and now*. Decide today that nothing is more important than living the life you were designed to live. Do not wait…Live now!

247

Left handers have it rough. The entire world is designed for right-handed people—watches, scissors, student desks, can openers, etc. This forces lefties to think creatively to adapt to their surroundings. As a left-hander Jimi Hendrix learned to play his guitar upside down. So when you find yourself playing by someone's rules, take it as an opportunity to be creative.

248

LEGACY: (L) Leave the world a better place than when you were born. (E) Enroll and energize others to do the same. (G) Give generously. (A) Act as if your life depends on it. (C) Communicate your vision to others. (Y) Yield to no obstacles. What is your LEGACY? Live it now!

249

Digital video recorders (DVRs) have a convenient feature: when you are watching live television, you can pause or rewind. So if you are distracted and miss something, you can simply rewind and replay the part of the show you missed. But in real life, there are no pause buttons or rewind buttons. If you miss a moment, it is gone forever. Live in the moment!

250

Henry Ward Beecher wrote, "Men's best successes come after their disappointments." Failure can be discouraging. But with each failure there is knowledge to be gained. With each failure there is the opportunity to grow stronger and more resilient. After each failure, success is one step closer.

251

In literature, there is an archetype called a threshold guardian. Its role is to test a person before he graduates to the next level of knowledge or awareness. As you make progress, life will test you. Life wants to know how much you want it. Success is not easy. Achievement is not convenient. No matter what challenges you face, you have exactly what it takes to overcome them.

252

There are those who do just enough to get by. They slip in just under the deadline. They put in just enough effort to get a passing grade. Then there are those who realize that just enough is not good enough. They excel in anything they commit themselves to doing. They constantly raise the bar to see just how high they can jump. Do not settle for just enough.

253

Mary Poole once said, "He who laughs, *lasts*." One of the keys to longevity is a sense of humor. A life without laughter is dull, flat, and boring. Whether you do it with a booming roar, an uncontrollable giggle, a goofy snort, an infectious chuckle, or a gasping-for-air cackle, add a healthy dose of laughter to your day—every day!

254

Someone once said, "I bargained with life for a penny, only to learn, dismayed, that any wage I would have asked of life, life would have paid." We get out of life what we ask and expect. Never sell yourself short. Your life is invaluable. Be unreasonable. Think big. Expect more. Demand more.

255

It is difficult to hear someone say that they are just killing time. Life is precious and every moment should be treasured. When you find yourself in a holding pattern—waiting on something or someone—make productive use of your free time. Call a relative or friend, read a book, create your to-do list. Do not squander the gift of time.

256

Zig Ziglar said, "Confidence is going after Moby Dick in a rowboat and taking the tartar sauce with you." However daunting the task... No matter how big the challenge... When the odds are stacked against you... Even when you are at your lowest point... Exude the confidence to accomplish whatever you wish.

257

Look at the words Terrific and Terrible. Only three letters separate them but they have very different meanings. But they are both derived from the same Latin root, meaning filled with fear. So, in a sense, they are distant cousins. But at some point Terrific chose a different path. No matter your past, you can choose your course going forward. If you are not happy with where you find yourself, be like Terrific and bring new meaning to your life!

258

Marcus Aurelius wrote, "Waste no more time arguing what a good man should be. Be one." It is easy to talk about what you should do, how you should act, and what you should say. But the most powerful example you can offer others is *being* the person you describe. Instead of describing and debating, be that person. This will have an impact that words will never have.

259

Henry James wrote, "It's time to start living the life you've imagined." What is holding you back? Do not wait for the perfect set of circumstances. That day will never come. Commit yourself today to begin to live the life of your dreams. And day by day, your dreams will become your reality!

260

It took me a while to get into foreign films with subtitles. I figured if I wanted to read, I would just read the book! But when I finally watched one, I realized what I had been missing. When you are not open to different points of view and trying new things, you miss out on what the world has to offer. Be open-minded.

261

Price Pritchett said, "Change always comes bearing gifts." It might be the gift of freedom. Perhaps it is the gift of a new perspective on life. Maybe it is the gift of an opportunity to build new skills. It could be the gift of releasing something that has been holding you back. No matter what package it is wrapped in, change will always bring a gift. Accept it!

262

Someone once said, "Everything will be okay in the end. If it is not okay, it is not the end." When you feel like giving up, keep going—it will be okay. When all is falling apart around you, keep going—it will be okay. In the end, it will be okay!

263

A lost job. An ended relationship. A health scare. In life there are significant events that are meant to serve as a wake-up call. But in response, most people do one of two things: they hit the snooze button or turn the alarm off. They ignore what life is trying to tell them. Do not sleep through life…wake up and listen to life's messages!

264

Frederick Douglass said, "If there is no struggling there is no progress." Throughout history many major accomplishments have been recorded. And the greater the achievement, the greater the challenges that had to be overcome. Improvement always involves a process—it is never automatic. In order to advance, some mountains have to be conquered. No struggle equals no progress.

265

Stephen Hawking observed, "I have noticed even people who claim that everything is predestined, and that we can do nothing to change it, look before they cross the road." On some level, everyone recognizes that they have some control or influence over their fate. Do everything you can do...and always look both ways before stepping out into the street.

266

There is an old proverb which goes, "A double-minded man is unstable in all his ways." It takes courage to stand up for your deeply-held beliefs. Resist the temptation to simply fit in and go with the crowd. Do not blow with the wind for the sake of popularity. Be crystal clear about your principles. Be single-minded in your convictions no matter who is around.

267

You are a work of art. You are a sculpture yet to be chiseled. You are a masterpiece yet to be painted. You are an epic yet to be written. You are a critically-acclaimed film yet to be produced. You are an award-winning play yet to be performed. The best in you is yet to come!

268

Erik Weihenmayer is one of a handful of people who has conquered the Seven Summits—reaching the highest peak on each of the seven continents. An amazing feat, right? Now consider the fact that he has been blind since he was 13 years old. Imagine the courage, will, and trust it takes to scale a mountain without sight. Though blind, he *sees* things most people never will.

269

Laurence Shames wrote, "Success and failure. We think of them as opposites, but they're really not. They're companions—the hero and the sidekick." In order to succeed, you will inevitably encounter some failures during your journey. Failure is a part of life. Cheer for the hero, but accept its sidekick!

270

Someone once said, "What matters the most should never give way to what matters the least." Many times it is the small stuff that can trip you up. When you focus on the trivial you lose sight of the important. Think of the countless hours people have wasted chasing insignificant things. Focus on what matters.

271

Everyone loves dimples. But a dimple is the result of an abnormally short zygomaticus major muscle. It pulls the center of the cheek and causes the indentation, which creates the dimple. Take your shortcomings and turn them into assets. Embrace your marvelous imperfections!

272

You are amazing. You are spectacular. You are marvelous. You are incredible. You are terrific. You are an original. You are a star. You are magnificent. You are a phenomenon. How do I know? I know what you are capable of. I know what is possible for you. I know the *true* you.

273

Lou Holtz said, "I can't believe that God put us on this earth to be ordinary." You came here for a specific reason. You were born to do amazing things. You are a gift to this world. You are unique in every way. You have talents that others cannot touch. You are not here to be ordinary. Be excellent! Be phenomenal! Be extraordinary!

274

Mediocre is a menace to magnificent. Average is the adversary of awesome. Fitting in is the foe of first-rate. Ordinary is the opponent of outstanding. Regular is the rival of remarkable. The norm is the nemesis of notable. Pick a side!

275

No matter how right you think you are, it is important to listen to another person's point of view. You can learn a lot by objectively considering others' thoughts and opinions. You never know...their perspective might transform you, benefit you, teach you, or inspire you. Listen.

276

Why color inside the lines when you can draw your own lines? Conventional wisdom tells us to follow established guidelines. It is a good thing the Wright Brothers did not color inside the lines. It is comforting to know that Dr. Daniel Hale Williams—who performed the first successful open-heart surgery—did not color inside the lines. Draw your own lines!

277

Someone once observed, "The nicest thing about the future is that it comes one day at a time." Your biggest goals in life can be realized by working toward them each day. The point at which your reality becomes your future is ultimately determined by you and the pace you set for yourself. Create your future—one day at a time.

278

Jim Rohn said, "How long should you try? Until." When you really want something, keep going until you get it. When you feel like giving in, keep going until the job is finished. When you recognize your purpose in life, keep going until it is fulfilled. When you have given your word, keep going until it is done. Keep going until...

279

Do you have any idea how much you are capable of? No one ever told you? It does not matter. Someone told you that you would not amount to anything? Who cares? You know better. It is that feeling deep down inside that is saying that there is more. Strive toward your potential. Awaken the greatness in you!

280

Albert Einstein said, "Many of the things you can count, don't count. Many of the things you can't count, really count." You cannot count friendship. You cannot count peace of mind. You cannot count a clear conscience. You cannot count encouraging someone. You cannot count happiness. You cannot count personal fulfillment. That is the stuff that *really* counts!

281

You make an impression within the first few seconds of meeting someone. Fair or not, conclusions are drawn about you. Do you greet strangers with a smile or smirk? Do you show more interest in them or yourself? Do you convey a sense of self-confidence or insecurity? Do not let your first impression be the last.

282

James Allen wrote, "The dreamers are the saviors of the world." Dreamers are the ones who refuse to accept things as they are. Dreamers are the ones who provide hope for tomorrow. Dreamers are the ones who have made the world a better place. Dreamers are the ones who see opportunities instead of obstacles. Be a dreamer—then make it happen.

283

Notice the similarity between the words comfort and conform. It is comfortable to conform to what everyone else is doing. Following the crowd is the easy route. It requires no thinking to be part of a herd. Demonstrate the courage it takes to chart your own course. Think for yourself. Be yourself. Be original. Be you.

284

A wise person once said, "Someday is not a day of the week." Someday I'll get a job that I actually enjoy. Someday I'll travel the world. Someday I'll pursue my purpose. Someday I'll tell them how I feel. Someday I'll take that course. Someday I'll give back to my community. Be specific and set a date for your someday.

285

Henry David Thoreau wrote, "The price of anything is the amount of life you exchange for it." So is it worth it...spending so much time engaged in that mindless activity? Is it worth it...refusing to speak to them for years because of that silly argument? You are bartering your life for everything you do. Make sure it is worth it.

286

Refuse to be a passenger in your own life. Do not gaze through the window as life quickly passes by. Do not wonder where you are heading next. Do not stay in bumper-to-bumper traffic going nowhere. Get behind the steering wheel. Set the GPS for your desired destination. Turn on your favorite tunes and let the top down. Take control of your life.

287

Harry Truman said, "It is amazing what you can accomplish if you do not care who gets the credit." When you are committed to doing good, you do not concern yourself with recognition. By jockeying for position and broadcasting your contributions, you waste valuable time that could have been better spent serving others. Give generously.

288

In his book *Outliers,* Malcolm Gladwell writes that the key to success in any field is practicing a particular task for at least 10,000 hours. This requires discipline and commitment to your craft. But here's the secret: when you are passionate about your work, those hours pass quickly. By the way, unless you are a TV critic, 10,000 hours of channel surfing does not count.

289

Mark Twain wrote, "Never argue with a fool. Onlookers may not be able to tell the difference." You have been there…having a debate with someone, and at some point you realize that they are not listening to a word you are saying. If they are not open to hearing your perspective, you will never convince them of anything. Choose your battles wisely!

290

Have you noticed the first minute of exercising is much easier than the last? The first mile of a marathon is always easier than the last. The first stretch of an all-day journey is lighter than the last. No matter how difficult it gets, do not give up in the final hour. Push through it and finish strong like the champion you are!

291

It has been said that you will always find someone who is better off than you and someone who is worse off. The key is not to be too proud when things are going well, and not to feel sorry for yourself when they are not. While there will always be others to compare yourself to, the only meaningful comparison is to your very best self.

292

Someone said, "Some people dream of success, while others wake up and work hard for it." The first step of any successful endeavor is imagining that it is possible. The second step is planning. The third step is executing that plan. Without action, your dream will remain just that—a dream. Work hard to make your dreams come true!

293

Dr. Julie vanPutten wrote, "Life is full of mystery, meaning, and magic. The challenge is to explore the mystery, discover the meaning, and create the magic in every moment." Notice life's clues as they appear before you. When you carefully piece them all together, you uncover the meaning of life—and the significance of yours. By living fully in the moment, you create life's magic. Only you hold the wand.

294

Get off the sidelines and into the game. Stop watching others play out their dreams on the field of life while you sit on the bench. Be the one the crowd is cheering on. Play offense by aggressively going after your goals. Play defense by guarding against the naysayers who will try to stop you from achieving your dreams. Get in the game!

295

Bob Proctor wrote, "It doesn't matter where you are, you are nowhere compared to where you can go." If you fully understood your potential, you would explore it. If you recognized your capability, you would not settle. If you realized that you have limitless possibilities within you, you would see each obstacle as temporary.

296

There is power in you greater than you could ever imagine. It has been there all along just waiting to be called forth. Just waiting to be unleashed. Just waiting to demonstrate its true strength. Just waiting to show everyone what you are made of. When you tap into your inner power, you can accomplish anything!

297

Someone once said, "Make your life a mission—not an intermission." The substance of every performance never takes place during intermission. In any game, halftime is not where the action happens. It is critical to take a break after working hard, but do not make that break permanent. Do not spend your life sitting idly by. Be on a mission!

298

Movies and television shows typically start with images of the setting in which the story takes place—whether shots of the countryside, skyline of a major city, or outer space. They do this to provide context for what you are about to see. Likewise, each decision you make should be made in the context of your purpose in life.

299

There is an old Chinese proverb which says, "A man who chases two rabbits goes home hungry." There is tremendous power in focusing. But that power is diluted when you try to do too many things at once. When you fully commit to what you want and focus your efforts, you accomplish so much more. Catch one rabbit now, then the next!

300

Diane Ackerman wrote, "I don't want to get to the end of my life and find that I lived just the length of it. I want to have lived the width of it as well." You cannot control the length of your life, but you can determine life's robustness. Not a trickle, but a powerful flow that occupies every inch of space that life offers. A life that is full of memorable experiences. A life that is greater than the years in your life due to the legacy you are creating. Live fully!

301

John E. Southard said, "The only people with whom you should try to get even are those who have helped you." There are two types of payback: one meant for good and one meant to harm. Getting revenge is a draining activity. Let go and move on. Spend your time and energy repaying the people who deserve it—the people who have made a difference in your life.

302

Imagine yourself giving the acceptance speech. So go ahead and write it. Visualize yourself winning the medal. So go ahead and practice hard like it is already yours. See yourself going on stage to receive the highest honor in your field. So go ahead and put in the extra effort. Believe in your heart that you can, then go make it a reality!

303

Og Mandino wrote, "Weak is he who permits his thoughts to control his actions; strong is he who forces his actions to control his thoughts." So many times people allow their thoughts and feelings to govern their behavior. But true strength is demonstrated when your actions have authority over your thoughts. Be strong and control your thoughts!

304

There is an African proverb that says, "The fly cannot be driven away by getting angry at it." Whenever you are in a situation you do not like, resist the temptation to get mad and sulk. Your anger alone will not resolve the situation. Channel that anger into productive action. Do not get mad...get to work.

305

Awaken the greatness within you. Act with urgency. Align with your life's purpose. Admit when you are wrong. Appreciate your loved ones. Assert yourself. Accept nothing but your best. Assume nothing. Admire people worthy of it. Adjust your attitude. Ask for support. Anticipate and adapt to change. Avoid negative people. Aspire to great things and achieve them.

306

Believe in yourself without fail. Build your future today. Breathe in and smell the roses. Baffle your critics with even more success. Begin with your goal in mind. Balance life and work. Bring about positive change. Breakdown barriers. Bring out the best in others. Burn the bridge—no escape routes. Bring solutions to problems. Bind your fear. Become who you were born to be.

———————◆———————

307

Create the life of your dreams. Consider different points of view. Care more. Control your anger. Cause a ripple effect. Collaborate with great minds. Convince yourself that you can—because you can. Cultivate positive relationships. Copy no one—you are an original. Check your ego at the door. Contribute to worthy causes. Compare yourself only to who you could be. Climb higher—the view is great.

———————◆———————

308

Dream big—no, even bigger. Dare to be different. Dance—even when everyone is looking. Do the right thing—even when no one is looking. Discover your life's purpose and pursue it passionately. Dive right in. Design the life you deeply desire. Draw on the infinite power inside you. Deliver on your word. Develop at least one new skill each year. Demand more out of life. Don't ever, ever give up!

309

Experience life's sweet moments. Empower, encourage, and energize others. Exhibit poise under pressure. Expand your vision. Exceed expectations. Embrace change. Engage in stimulating conversations. Exercise your mind, body, and spirit. Envy no one. Exit your comfort zone. Earn others' respect. Envision yourself achieving that goal. Epitomize excellence.

310

Face your potential—it has been staring at you for far too long. Fear nothing. Find ten reasons to keep going. Follow great leaders. Free yourself. Finish the job. Fail in order to succeed. Figure it out—there is always a solution. Feel good. Fan the flames of success. Fight for your beliefs. Fantasize, then make it a reality. Focus on the stuff that matters. Fly higher.

311

Go with a different kind of flow. Gather evidence about how amazing you are. Greet each new day as a gift. Give generously. Get going on your dreams. Go ahead. Generate enthusiasm. Grab a great opportunity with both hands. Govern your thoughts—not vice versa. Grow from each mistake. Give up on the idea that you cannot—you can. Go for it!

312

Hope that your dreams come true—then do what is necessary to make them so. Hold yourself to a higher standard. Hush the naysayers. Hang in there—this, too, shall pass. Hasten to your goals. Hop to it. Handle adversity with grace. Hunt for a better way. Help yourself, then others. Hum daily. Heighten your awareness to the opportunities around you. Hear this: You are phenomenal!

313

Imagine… Instigate a riot of excellence and ignite the fire of enthusiasm. Intensify your efforts. Inspire those around you. Increase your reach. Invent your future. Ignore chronically negative people. Improvise when things do not go as planned. Instill confidence in others. Invest in your own development. Imitate no one. Inflict kindness. Issue this proclamation: I can do anything!

314

Juice life like an orange—squeeze out every single drop. Join the chorus of possibility. Juggle your priorities. Jazz up each day with excitement. Journey to your infinite potential. Justify your existence by doing good. Joke around. Jettison all unneeded baggage. Jam-pack your surroundings with positive, uplifting people. Jog through it. Jump to it.

315

Know this: You are incredible! Kick down the door to the life of your dreams. Kick start your brilliant future. Kiss the chains of the past goodbye. Kindle a fire of hope. Keep your chin up—your day will come. Kill off negative beliefs. Key in to who you were born to be. Knight yourself—you are noble.

316

Live fully. Laugh often. Love freely. Learn to be a lifelong learner. Lead courageously. Listen openly. Lighten up. Let go. Lift off to new heights. Look forward, not behind. Live by your word and for something meaningful. Leave that stuff in the past. Lift others up. Latch on to great ideas. Light up the world with your smile!

317

Maximize what works and minimize what does not. Maintain a positive outlook. Move whatever gets in your way. Multiply your power. Master your thoughts. Mentor someone. Mobilize others. Mix it up. Model extraordinary behaviors. Meet at least three new people each day. Motivate those around you. Measure up to your potential. Map the course. Make this world a better place.

318

Name yourself MVP of your life. Nail down what you want. Negotiate life's unexpected curves with confidence. Notify the world that you are a force to be reckoned with. Nurture your dreams until they become a reality. Neutralize negativity. Navigate wisely to your destination. Net the big fish—with a bigger net. Narrate the story of the life you deserve. Never, ever give up!

319

Outdo today what you did yesterday. Open the door when opportunity knocks. Operate at a higher level of performance. Ooze self-confidence. Outpace your competition. Overcome every obstacle. Offer a hand of support. Own your voice. Order dessert first. Optimize your time. Observe what is going on around you. Orchestrate a comeback.

320

Participate fully in life. Play like you mean it. Pick up the pace. Pull out all the stops. Pursue your purpose with passion. Preserve your integrity. Prioritize the stuff that matters. Perfect nothing—because nothing is perfect. Prune the dead branches in your life. Pack your bags and move on. Provoke others into their greatness. Prepare, perform, persevere, and prevail!

321

Quiver at the thought of your potential—it is just that awesome. Quote great minds. Quench your thirst for knowledge. Question everything at least once. Quarantine yourself from pessimists. Quick-freeze the words *I can't*—and keep them on ice. Quantify the difference you make. Quicken your pace. Quilt together a terrific life. Quadruple your efforts—then do it again!

322

Realize this: You are amazing! Recognize the vast power you have within you. Reach higher, wider, and further. Recruit superstars into your life. Rev-up your engine. Release your past—it is dragging you down. Remain calm in spite of your circumstances. Read and grow. Reward yourself—you earned it. Renew, reinvigorate, and revitalize yourself. Raise the bar—even higher!

323

Smile—and just watch the reaction you get. Search for the greatness in everyone you meet. Silence your inner critic. Summon your magnificent self to step forth. Settle for nothing less than what you deserve—and you deserve the best. Speak up. Set yourself up for success. Stare down obstacles. Spice up your life. Simplify everything. Serve others. So what are you waiting for? Start now!

324

Tick off naysayers by doing the impossible. Take your life more seriously than you take yourself. Treat others with dignity. Tap into the wisdom of those around you. Tear down the walls that are holding you back. Transform the world—starting with yourself. Tell them how you feel. Take off and climb higher. Transmit optimism everywhere you go. Turn the corner—your future is waiting.

325

Upset the apple cart—it is time to shake things up. Uncover your life's purpose. Urge others toward their greatness. Uncork your potential—it is dying to get out. Upgrade to a first-class life. Unwrap and utilize fully the gifts you have been given. Uplift others. Undertake a worthy cause. Utter these words every day: I can do anything!

326

Veer off the well-traveled path to discover your own. Visualize yourself achieving your biggest dreams. Vanquish fear. Venture outside your comfort zone. Validate others' points of view. Voice your opinion with conviction. Value diversity of thought. View each day as a gift. Volunteer. Vote. Vie for a winning life. Vow to live up to the possibilities you have within.

327

Weather the storms of life. Worry not. Watch others, learn from them, and do even better. Widen your vision for your life. Welcome your bright future. Woo everyone with your enthusiasm. Work smart—play hard. Whistle. Wipe the slate clean. Witness a miracle each day—they are all around you. Win with integrity. Write the fairytale ending to your life's story—you hold the pen.

328

X out negativity—try optimism. X out small-mindedness—dream big. X out playing it safe—be outrageous. X out living someone else's dreams—live your dreams. X out self-imposed limits—imagine endless possibilities. X out the chains of the past—usher in the bright future. X out arrogance—try humility. X out mediocrity—be excellent.

329

Yearn to be the absolute best you can be. Yield to no obstacle, to no hurdle, to no barrier, to no challenge. Yawn in the face of adversity. Yank life lessons from each success—and each failure. Yell this declaration: It is a wonderful life. You can do it! Yes, you can!

330

Zero in on what you truly want. Zone out when pessimists get on a roll. Zap the energy out of naysayers with perpetual positivity. Zero out the odds when they are stacked against you. Zoom out to see the big picture. Zigzag through life by collecting rich and diverse experiences. Zip to the life of your dreams—you deserve it!

331

Since 1936 only twelve college football teams have had the Heisman Trophy winner (the highest honor bestowed upon a college football player) on their team and won the national title in the same season. A team can have the very best player in the nation, but that is not enough to win the championship. A strong team will always go further than a lone star player.

332

Warren Bennis once wrote, "Excellence is a better teacher than mediocrity. The lessons of the ordinary are everywhere. Truly profound insights are to be found only in studying the exemplary." Ordinary is pervasive. Excellence is rare. Ordinary is commonplace. Excellence is uncommon. What examples are you studying—the ordinary or the excellent?

333

Robert Schuller once asked, "What would you attempt to do if you knew you could not fail?" Recall the feeling you have when you are about to do something you have mastered…something you could do with your eyes closed. That is the mindset with which you should walk through life. Fear of failure is the main thing that holds most people back. Imagine if failure were not possible. What would you do that you have not done?

334

Albert Einstein wrote, "Imagination is more important than knowledge." Do you remember how, as a kid, you would spend time imagining? No limitations. No reality checks. Not imprisoned by logic. Just pure, uninhibited imagination. When you allow yourself to think freely and creatively you open endless possibilities. Just imagine…

335

An unexpected roadblock is an opportunity to experience a different path. A failed attempt is an opportunity to discover a better way. A seemingly impossible challenge is an opportunity to grow stronger. A setback is an opportunity to regroup then forge ahead. Show me your problem and I will introduce you to your opportunity.

336

Les Brown said, "Life has no limitations, except the ones you make." Consider the people throughout history who have overcome huge challenges in order to become successful. They created a vision that was bigger than their circumstances. Self-imposed, limiting beliefs have held back more people than any other obstacle. Open the door that is holding you back. You have the key.

337

William Shakespeare wrote, "Boldness, be my friend." Boldness empowers you to dream beyond the limited imagination of others. Boldness allows you to step past your fears to do what you really want. Boldness enables you to speak up for important causes. Make Boldness your friend!

338

A study was done on the shortage of available taxicabs on rainy afternoons in a major city. People assumed that cabs were not available because more people were using them. While that was true to some extent, the study revealed that there actually were fewer cabs than on clear afternoons. This was because, on rainy days, once the cab drivers met their targets (earlier than usual), most went home for the day. The lesson: When you achieve your goals, take time to celebrate your success. Then go back and achieve your next goal!

339

Marian Wright Edelman said, "Service is the rent we pay for the space we take up on earth." Nothing is free. In order to have a life of meaning, you must focus outward. In order to have a life of significance, you must give back. Is the world a better place because you are in it? Pay your rent—serve others!

340

What is that over there in the corner? It looks as though it has been sitting there for a very long time. It appears that it has not been used for years. Even though it is dusty its brilliance is peeking through. Look! There is a tag on it saying that it belongs exclusively to you. It is the bundle of gifts and natural talents you were endowed with when you were born. Use your gifts!

341

Longinus wrote, "In great attempts, it is glorious even to fail." One of the biggest mistakes people make in life is aiming low and playing it safe. Great things can only be accomplished through great attempts. Typically, the higher the risk, the greater the potential reward. Play big!

342

Samuel Goldwyn said, "The harder I work, the luckier I get." Hard work pays off. In the vast majority of cases luck comes to those who are prepared to benefit from it. When you work hard, you are able to recognize great opportunities and capitalize on them. If you want to change your luck, work harder!

343

When you fail to show your appreciation to others, you prevent them from knowing the impact they have made on your life. Your silence suggests that you take them for granted. Thinking "I do not have to say anything, because they know how I feel" is a cop-out. They only truly know how you feel when you say so. Do not be stingy with praise and gratitude. Give thanks…out loud.

344

You do not know when this movie called life will end, so focus on what takes place before the credits roll. You have the power to write the rest of your script. Redefine the role you will play. Choose the characters who play a part in your life. Decide if it is dramatic, funny, tragic, or uplifting. Determine if it is a blockbuster or straight-to-video. You have the power to create the story of your dreams.

345

"When things go wrong as they sometimes will,
When the road you're trudging seems all uphill,
When the funds are low and the debts are high,
And you want to smile, but you have to sigh,
When care is pressing you down a bit –
Rest if you must, but don't quit."
  - From the poem *Don't Quit*
No matter what you have gone through or what you are currently going through, do not give up. In the short run, it is easier to call it quits. But perseverance pays off when you reap the benefits of your hard work. Don't quit!

346

Years ago I read a book about a company I was working with at the time. Throughout the years, the book's title has stuck with me: "Control Your Destiny or Someone Else Will." These words have served as a guiding principle for my life. You have the power to create your future or you can give that power to someone else. Ultimately, the choice is yours. Control your destiny.

347

T.L. Kirkland said, "A test is designed to determine where the student stands." Everything serves a purpose. Sometimes life presents you with a situation to test you. Once you pass that test, you move on to the next one. If you find yourself facing the same circumstances or challenges over and over again, ask yourself how you are responding. Change your response until you pass the test!

348

There are few things as strong as a powerful dream—a vision so life-like you can almost see, touch, taste, smell, and hear it. Everything you see around you (houses, cars, billboards, traffic lights, trains, buses, etc.) was first imagined by someone. When your dream is accompanied by your unwavering commitment to making it a reality, nothing can stop you. Follow your dreams.

349

Marilyn Ferguson wrote, "Our past is not our potential. In any hour, you can choose to liberate the future." So many people believe that they are prisoners of their past. It does not matter what your story is. It does not matter what you went through to get where you are. It does not matter what obstacles you had to overcome. Let go of the stuff that has been holding you back. Free yourself!

350

Have you ever reconnected with someone whom you had not seen in years and after speaking with them you realized how much you have changed, while they seem exactly the same? Not externally, but internally. Their perspective, conversation, and priorities are all the same. It is almost as if they have been frozen in time. You are different, but they are the same. This simply means you have been growing and developing. Keep progressing!

351

Euripides, the Greek playwright, once wrote, "Time will explain it all. He is a talker, and needs no questioning before he speaks." When you are going through a difficult situation, it can be very hard to understand why it is happening. You may ask *Why me?* or *Why now?* But everything happens for a reason. With the benefit of hindsight, you gain perspective. Time explains all things.

352

At times you can spend so much time hanging on that you do not realize that what you really need to do is let go. What are you holding on to that is not working for your good? Let go of limited beliefs. Let go of the past. Let go of it all. Let go and be open to the blessings in store for you.

353

Howard Thurman wrote, "You must ask yourself two questions: First, Where am I going in life? Second, Who's going with me? And if you get the questions in the wrong order, you're in big trouble." Just think of the tragic stories of people "hanging with the wrong crowd." The people with whom you associate should be a reflection of where you are going, not the other way around. Where first…who next.

354

John Wooden said, "Reputation is what others think you are. Character is what you really are. I believe that character is much more important." It is easy to fall into the trap of focusing on what others think about you, sometimes at the expense of your character. In spite of all the pressure, always be true to yourself. Place character over reputation.

355

Looking at the world's challenges, it is tempting to become overwhelmed and throw up your hands in defeat. Never underestimate the power one person can have. As the old proverb says, "A small rudder can steer a huge ship." Dr. Martin Luther King, Jr. was only one person, but his life and leadership changed the course of the most powerful nation on earth. You have immense power within you. Use it.

356

Eleanor Roosevelt said, "Nobody can make you feel inferior without your consent." You have the power to choose a response to everything that happens to you—to every word that is spoken to you. If someone suggests that they are somehow superior to you, you have to give them permission before he or she can occupy that position. Never allow another person's opinion of you to define you.

357

Oprah Winfrey said, "Lots of people want to ride with you in the limo, but what you want is someone who will take the bus with you when the limo breaks down." There is absolutely nothing like a true friend. Someone who sees you, not for what you have, but for who you are. Someone who keeps you grounded when things are going well…and sits by you when they are not.

358

How will you be remembered? Will you be remembered for taking or giving? Will you be remembered for your sense of style or your sense of dignity? Will you be remembered for making others feel small or for urging them into their greatness? Will you be remembered for living a life of obscurity or creating a legacy? How will you be remembered?

359

Calvin Coolidge said, "Christmas is not a time nor a season, but a state of mind. To cherish peace and goodwill, to be plenteous in mercy, is to have the real spirit of Christmas." During the holidays, it is amazing to see the numerous acts of generosity: people volunteering, shoppers opening the door for others, donations being made to those in need, warm smiles and cheerful greetings. Allow your "better self" to be on display, not only during the holiday season, but each day of the year.

360

D.M. Dellinger said, "You are unrepeatable. There is a magic about you that is all your own..." You are an original. There is no one on earth like you. You are the special sauce on life's burger. Your smile is uniquely yours. You have gifts and talents that no one else can offer. You have power beyond your imagination. You are something else. You are unrepeatable!

361

Voltaire wrote, "The best way to become boring is to say everything." You can hear them coming from miles away—those who try to dominate every moment of a conversation. However, the most interesting people are those who show an interest in you. Ask questions. Share the spotlight. Engage in conversation, not a presentation. Communication is a two-way street.

362

Someone said, "A shin is a device used to find furniture in the dark." In life, everyone gets some bumps and bruises. They may come in the form of failures, mistakes, disappointments, missteps, upsets, hurt feelings, or plans gone awry. The important thing is that you keep going even when you cannot see the entire path. At the end of every night there is daylight.

363

Aristotle wrote, "It is the mark of a wise mind to be able to entertain a thought without accepting it." Considering someone's opinion is not only showing them respect, it is also a sign of wisdom. Never believe that you know everything there is to know. Genuinely consider a belief or point of view with which you do not initially agree. Entertain the thought!

364

Norman Cousins wrote, "No one really knows enough to be a pessimist." In order to honestly say that something cannot be done, a pessimist has to try every approach and fail. They must be creative enough to think of all other possible approaches, try them all, and fail. They also have to know the capabilities of every person who will come along after them to try to do what they could not. Who knows that much?

365

I know that your very best stuff is still in you. It is your star player who is anxiously waiting on the bench for the coach to put him in the game. It is your show's headliner waiting backstage for the opening act to wrap up so she can take the stage. It is your entrée being kept warm in the kitchen waiting for you to finish the appetizer. Bring out your very best. Live A Phenomenal Life!

APPENDIX

DAY OF YEAR NUMBER CONVERSION

	Jan	Feb	Mar	Apr	May	Jun
1	1	32	60	91	121	152
2	2	33	61	92	122	153
3	3	34	62	93	123	154
4	4	35	63	94	124	155
5	5	36	64	95	125	156
6	6	37	65	96	126	157
7	7	38	66	97	127	158
8	8	39	67	98	128	159
9	9	40	68	99	129	160
10	10	41	69	100	130	161
11	11	42	70	101	131	162
12	12	43	71	102	132	163
13	13	44	72	103	133	164
14	14	45	73	104	134	165
15	15	46	74	105	135	166
16	16	47	75	106	136	167
17	17	48	76	107	137	168
18	18	49	77	108	138	169
19	19	50	78	109	139	170
20	20	51	79	110	140	171
21	21	52	80	111	141	172
22	22	53	81	112	142	173
23	23	54	82	113	143	174
24	24	55	83	114	144	175
25	25	56	84	115	145	176
26	26	57	85	116	146	177
27	27	58	86	117	147	178
28	28	59	87	118	148	179
29	29		88	119	149	180
30	30		89	120	150	181
31	31		90		151	
	Jan	Feb	Mar	Apr	May	Jun

DAY OF YEAR NUMBER CONVERSION (CONTINUED)

	Jul	Aug	Sep	Oct	Nov	Dec
1	182	213	244	274	305	335
2	183	214	245	275	306	336
3	184	215	246	276	307	337
4	185	216	247	277	308	338
5	186	217	248	278	309	339
6	187	218	249	279	310	340
7	188	219	250	280	311	341
8	189	220	251	281	312	342
9	190	221	252	282	313	343
10	191	222	253	283	314	344
11	192	223	254	284	315	345
12	193	224	255	285	316	346
13	194	225	256	286	317	347
14	195	226	257	287	318	348
15	196	227	258	288	319	349
16	197	228	259	289	320	350
17	198	229	260	290	321	351
18	199	230	261	291	322	352
19	200	231	262	292	323	353
20	201	232	263	293	324	354
21	202	233	264	294	325	355
22	203	234	265	295	326	356
23	204	235	266	296	327	357
24	205	236	267	297	328	358
25	206	237	268	298	329	359
26	207	238	269	299	330	360
27	208	239	270	300	331	361
28	209	240	271	301	332	362
29	210	241	272	302	333	363
30	211	242	273	303	334	364
31	212	243		304		365
	Jul	Aug	Sep	Oct	Nov	Dec

ABOUT THE AUTHOR

CLIFTON ANDERSON, JR. has been called "one of the most profound thinkers of his generation." He is a gifted results coach, author, speaker, and a relentless believer in human potential. He has an amazing ability to bring out the very best in people and help them create phenomenal results in their lives. Prior to pursuing his purpose of inspiring and empowering others, Clifton—at the age of 37—was named Chief Financial Officer (CFO) of a $1.5 billion global company headquartered in Southern California. He has worked with some of the most respected companies, organizations, and universities. As a former senior executive, he now shares the secrets that propelled him to an outstanding record of achievement and success. Clifton holds an MBA from the prestigious Wharton School of the University of Pennsylvania. He has traveled to over thirty countries and visited six of the seven continents.

To learn more about Clifton and for information on other
products and services, visit his website:
www.clifton-anderson.com

Live A Phenomenal Life™